LEASING
The Accounting & Taxation Implications

by David Wainman C.A.
& Howard Brown A.C.A.
Partners, Whinney Murray & Co.

GUILD PRESS

PREFACE

How to account for leases has long been recognised as a complex problem. It may not be unfair to say that, with the growth of leasing, it has recently become more problematical, as those holding opposing views entrench themselves more belligerently. This book is an attempt to examine their viewpoints objectively. We have reached our own conclusions, and we indicate what these are. But they are conclusions reached from an open-minded starting point, as a result of our studies.

Tax is a study all on its own, but in relation to leasing it must be recognised as an integral part of the central battleground.

We are grateful to numerous colleagues for assistance, in particular to John Munro and Jorge Kin. Our conclusions, however, are our own and do not necessarily coincide with those of our colleagues or represent the views of our firm.

26th September 1978

DPW
HRB

Published by
GUILD PRESS
Park Place House, Tunnel Street, St. Helier, Jersey.

ISBN 0 9505174 53

Printed by JEP-Lithoprint (Jersey) Ltd.

CONTENTS

CHAPTER 1 – INTRODUCTION

Contents

DEFINITION OF A LEASE

1.01 A lease can be defined as a contract between the owner and the hirer for the letting of a specific asset. This contract constitutes what is legally known as a contract of bailment. It conveys the right to use the asset from the owner to the lessee for a specified period of time. The lessee thus obtains possession and use for the lease term unless there occurs some major breach which enables one party or other to terminate the contract prematurely. The lessee pays a specified rent to the lessor for possession and use. Throughout the lease, the lessor retains legal ownership of the leased asset. The lease does not normally in the UK confer on the lessee either the right or the obligation to acquire the asset during the lease term or thereafter.

1.02 Many variants have been devised to satisfy the differing needs of lessors and lessees but all have in common the fundamental characteristic of segregating use from ownership. It is this characteristic which distinguishes leasing from other methods of financing such as mortgaging.

OPERATING LEASES

1.03 Leases are normally differentiated as being either operating leases or finance leases. The single factor distinguishing these classes more clearly than any other is the lessor's view of his activity. Does he regard himself as lending money in order to make profit in the form of interest or does he regard himself as operating an asset in order to make profit from it?

An operating lease has the following characteristics:

a) the profit which emerges depends to a significant extent upon the lease-end asset value;

b) the lease term covers only a part of the anticipated useful life of the asset, and the lessor therefore does not amortize it fully in his books during that term;

c) the lessor is usually responsible for maintenance and insurance of the leased asset;

d) the lease agreement may require the lessor to accept back the leased asset prematurely without a major penalty being imposed upon the lessee.

One can perhaps summarise by saying that the lessor retains substantially all the benefits and risks associated with the ownership of his property.

FINANCE LEASES

1.04 The characteristics of a finance or "full pay-out" lease are the antithesis of those listed above, in that:-

a) The profit which emerges is not dependent to a significant extent upon the value to the lessor of the leased asset at the end of the lease term;

b) Because the lease covers substantially the whole anticipated useful life of the asset its written down value in the books of the lessor by the end of the lease term is small in relation to the original cost. Only where the asset will be fully amortized by the end of the term is a finance lease strictly a "full pay-out lease" but these expressions are normally synonymous, and are used interchangeably in what follows.

c) The lessee is usually responsible for maintenance and insurance of the leased asset;

d) Finance lease agreements frequently contain a clause penalising the lessee if he causes premature termination, by requiring from him as a minimum a payment to ensure that the lessor's implicit rate of return is maintained. Currently there is some doubt over the extent to which the courts would enforce a clause whose terms were penal, and it is thought that such a clause should reflect the anticipated sale proceeds for the asset in the charge made to the lessee.

Summarising once again, it can be said that a finance lease effectively conveys most of the benefits and risks of ownership to the lessee. There are, however, two important areas where this principle does not apply.

STATUTORY OBLIGATIONS

1.05 Firstly there are certain statutory responsibilities which cannot be shrugged off by the lessor. For instance, he cannot transfer to the lessee his obligations under the Health and Safety at Work legislation. These purely legal aspects of the leasing relationship are not dealt with in this work.

TAX LEGISLATION

1.06 Secondly there is the constraint arising primarily from fiscal legislation which prevents the lessor from giving the lessee all the economic benefit. We will return to this both in its accounting and taxation aspects, but the principles can be briefly noted at this point. It is common practice for a substantial proportion of the disposal proceeds of an asset, after the end of a finance lease term, to be paid over by the lessor to the lessee "by way of rebate of hire". The lessor has achieved the profit he sought in the form of an "interest" element included in the rent and he now regards the lessee as having "paid for" the asset. But he cannot go so far as to say that, at the end of the lease term, the lessee has acquired a title which he did not have before, because it is of the essence of leasing as understood in the UK, and particularly in UK tax, that the lessee does not have the right to acquire the asset. However the lessor, whilst retaining his own rights to the asset, beneficially and legally, does go some way towards admitting a "participation" by the lessee. One form of admission is that indicated above; if the asset is sold, a substantial part of the proceeds is passed to the lessee as a rebate of rent. Another form, where the lessee continues to rent the asset is to reduce the rent to a nominal amount in the secondary period, that is, after the expiry of the "primary" lease term.

GUIDELINES FOR DIFFERENTIATING FINANCE LEASES FROM OPERATING LEASES

1.07 Because of the different risks inherent for the lessor in finance as opposed to operating leases, different methods are used to determine the appropriate pattern of the lessor's profits through the lease.

Differentiating the types of lease therefore becomes vital. There are no rules laid down in the UK specifying what is a finance lease and what is an operating lease, but, while inevitably there will be cases close to the dividing line, in our view a lease which fulfils one of the following conditions should normally be regarded as a finance lease:-

a) The lease term covers a major portion, say 75%, of the anticipated useful life of the asset;

b) The anticipated lease rents, discounted at the interest rate implicit in the lease to their present value, equate to, say, 90% of the asset's value at that time;

This second condition needs refinement in many cases. The anticipated lease rents should perhaps be the rents stated in the lease after allowing for any rebate anticipated if the asset is sold at the end of the lease term. Similarly, the values to the lessor of grants received towards the asset's purchase, and of tax reliefs received for that asset, also need to be taken into consideration.

HIRE PURCHASE AND LEASES WITH PURCHASE OPTIONS

1.08 The fundamental characteristic of a lease has already been stated— the separation of use from ownership. There fall within this definition not only the finance and operating leases we have been considering, but also leases with a right or option for the lessee to purchase the asset. Hire purchase is one example of the lease with an option.

The consideration stipulated for the acquisition, whether obligatory or optional, can vary between a nominal sum and an open market price. An option to purchase at a figure well below market price is often referred to as a bargain purchase option.

1.09 This distinction between a lease where the lessee has the right to receive substantially all the proceeds arising from the sale of the leased asset at the end of the lease term and one where the lessee has the right to buy the asset at that time for a nominal consideration is important because of the differing tax treatment.

GROWTH OF LEASING

1.10 The concept of segregating the use of an asset from its ownership is not new. Leasing of land has a very long and well documented history. But the real growth in the UK of plant leasing has taken place only in the last ten years. The value of UK assets, other than real property, subject to lease in 1967 was estimated at £20m. Today the figure is probably £3,000m.

GENERAL ADVANTAGES

1.11 The advantages of leasing, which have given rise to this explosive growth are many. Looked at simply as a form of financing, leasing can offer the following advantages:-

a) Most leases provide 100% medium term finance at a fixed rate;

b) The borrowing involved in a finance lease is currently, in the UK, not accounted for on the lessee's balance sheet. The lessee not only avoids difficulties he might otherwise experience in areas such as the borrowing limits laid down in his Articles of Association, or in his debenture trust deed; he also preserves in full his ability to raise funds from his existing lines of credit, and his ability to issue shares by rights issues or by public or private placings.

(c) Documentation is not only simpler but often more flexible than is the case with other forms of borrowing.

ADVANTAGES FLOWING FROM TAX BASED LEASING

1.12 However it is the tax benefit that has been the major reason for leasing's enormous growth. In what is generally referred to as "tax based leasing":-

a) The lessor will normally be able to take immediate advantage of 100% tax allowances, whereas not every lessee could absorb them, perhaps through low profitability, coupled with stock appreciation relief and other capital allowances;

The advantage to the lessor shows up in a reduction in his own need for finance, as soon as he receives the benefit of tax liabilities reduced by those 100% allowances. He can therefore pass some part of his savings of financing costs to the lessee, in the rents which he is able to quote.

b) This benefit will usually produce for the lessee a better cash flow—at least in the early years of the lease;

c) It will also, in those early years, normally mean that the rent which the lessee charges against his profits, under current accounting practice, will be less than the amounts which he would need to charge for interest and depreciation were he himself to purchase the asset.

All of these are matters which we will re-examine and quantify in subsequent chapters of this book.

MATTERS NOT DEALT WITH IN THIS BOOK

1.13 What we will not be dealing with are:-

a) Value added tax;

b) Exchange control, either that operated by the Bank of England, or by other regulatory authorities for territories other than the UK;

c) Overseas taxes, either in relation to a UK taxpayer who may to some extent be able to obtain credit against his UK liabilities for those overseas taxes paid; or in relation to the combined effects of overseas and UK taxes on a non-UK based person who is operating in the UK.

From the second and third of these exclusions it will be clear that we are not attempting to deal with "cross-border" leasing. We concentrate on UK lessors and lessees, looking outside our own boundaries only in relation to their operations in currencies, (paragraph 3.24 et seq,) and for a comparison of our accounting methods with those used in the U.S. (Chapter 6).

CHAPTER 2 – THE LESSOR'S ACCOUNTS

Contents

ACCOUNTING FOR FINANCE LEASES

2.01 There are several methods, each commanding some degree of acceptance, of accounting for finance lease income and of describing the asset and quantifying the amount at which it is to be stated in the lessor's accounts:-

a) the straight-line method;

b) the market value method;

c) the annuity method;

d) the rule of 78, (and the reverse rule of 78);

e) the investment period method;

2.02 In this chapter we outline these five methods and using a simple example demonstrate how widely different are the various results. The chart below summarises in pictorial form these differing results from this same example. The total length of each horizontal length of line represents an amount of lease rent receivable in each year, that rent being at a level amount throughout a five year lease. The bars eating into this total income from the left hand margin represent the lessor's interest expense and doubtful debt provisions. Bars extending into total income from the right hand margin represent the lessor's provision for depreciation of the asset. Where these two sets of bars fall short of each other, the gap in the middle is the profit for the year. Where the bars overlap each other, that overlap is the loss for the year.

The chart shows plainly that the different accounting conventions produce widely different patterns of profit and loss through the five year period. So widely different that it is easy not to appreciate that the aggregate profit for the whole period remains unaltered despite the differences in the timing of its recognition.

CHART ILLUSTRATING THE RESULTS OF THE DIFFERENT METHODS

2.03

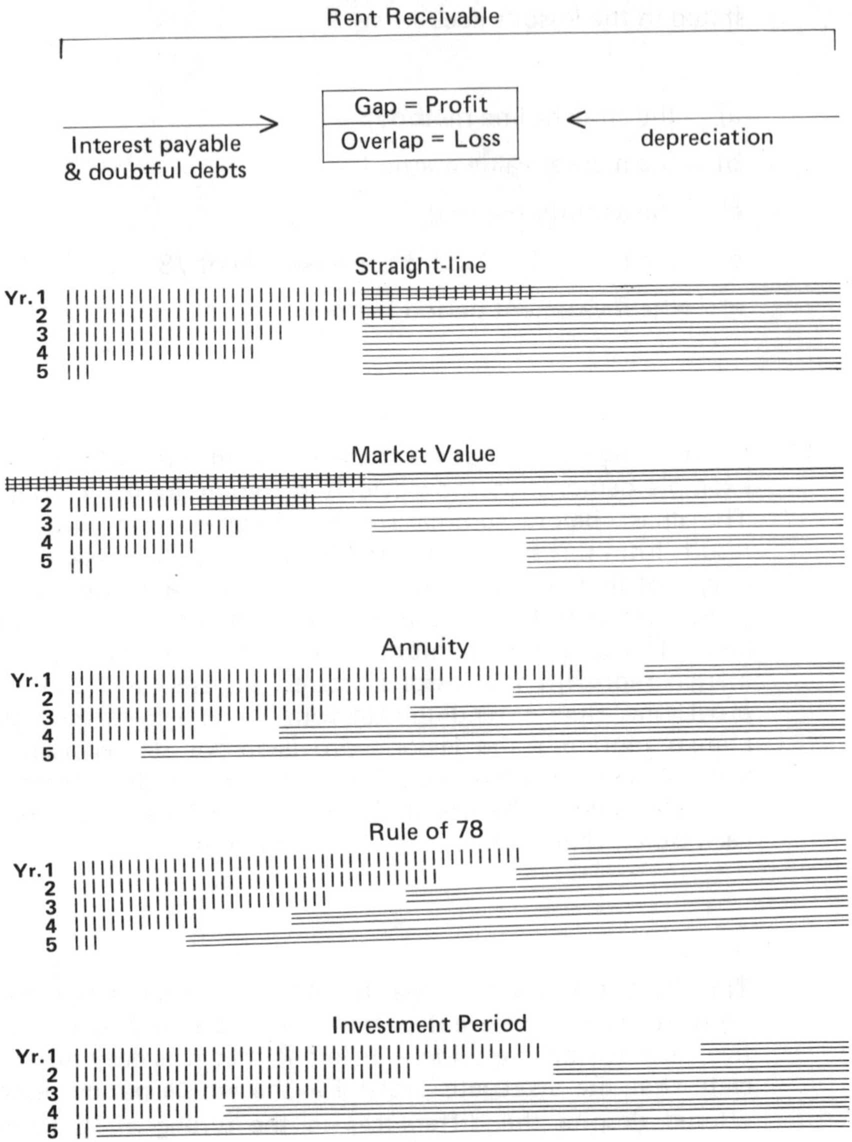

"CASH INVESTED IN THE LEASE"

2.04 The chart also brings out another relationship. The "value" put on the leased asset at any balance sheet date during the five year period is equal to the aggregate amount of the depreciation to be provided in the years following that date, plus any residual value anticipated. This figure usually appears in the lessor's balance sheet described as a fixed asset.

If he has borrowed money in order to provide all or part of the purchase price of that fixed asset, then there will appear on the liabilities side of his balance sheet the amount of this borrowing, so far as he has not repaid it by the relevant balance sheet date. Our basic example is worked on the basis that all the necessary funds are borrowed, and that each year's rental income is utilised primarily to pay interest on that borrowing, but thereafter to reduce its amount. The outstanding borrowing at any given date is referred to as the "cash invested in the lease," this being a phrase which we will be meeting repeatedly in what follows.

What we should notice at this juncture is that there is no reason why the "value" of the asset should be equal to that of the cash invested in the lease at any date after the commencement of the lease period. In fact there is every reason why they should differ.

"RECOGNITION OF PROFIT"

2.05 The difference between the asset "value" and the cash invested in the lease can be thought of, in balance sheet, terms as comprising two main items:-

a) The credit balance on the provision for doubtful debts. We will explain in paragraph 2.10 below the basis upon which such a provision is usually created and maintained. It is reasonable to regard this provision as a liability, not as a reserve. It is in this sense distinct from the next item.

b) Shareholders funds. Assuming that the whole cost of the fixed asset was finance by borrowing, this will be the cumulative profit to date to the extent that it has not been distributed.

In describing the "balancing" of the balance sheet in this way, we are approaching the fundamental meaning of profit—it is simply the balancing item, the amount by which assets exceed liabilities. Secondly, we can see that if the liabilities fall faster than the values of the assets, we will be "recognising" increased amounts of profit at each year end. Once again the phrase "recognition of profit" is one which we will meet repeatedly throughout this book. It denotes the way in which the total profit arising from the lease is allocated between the accounting periods over which the lease extends. It also reminds us that the amount of profit which can be recognised at any year end is dependent, mainly, on the "value" put on the asset; or in other words the level of the depreciation charge is the main determining factor.

THE RISK AND THE COVER FOR THAT RISK

2.06 Looking again at the figures which will appear in each year's balance sheet, we can draw out another relationship.

a) The lessor's gross risk at any time is the amount he owes to the provider of his loan capital—the amount we have described as the "cash invested in the lease".

b) Against that he has "cover" in the form of the asset which has a net realisable value which could be put towards paying off the creditor should the lessee default, and the lease therefore be terminated.

It will normally be the case that the net difference between these two items will decrease through the lease period. We can express this another way by saying that the lessor's net risk, as well as his gross risk, can be expected to decrease as the lease progresses. There is therefore a reasonable argument for saying that greater amounts of profit should be recognised early in the lease period when the risk is greatest, and that therefore profits could be expected to decline as risk also reduces.

THE BASIC EXAMPLE

2.07 We will now turn to the example illustrated in the chart in paragraph 2.03.

A lessor company has acquired an asset costing £100,000 and is letting it on a full payout basis for five years, the quarterly rent payable in advance being £7,100. The whole of the finance for the asset purchase has been borrowed by the lessor, at 3½% per quarter on the outstanding balance, and rental receipts are wholly utilised in paying interest and reducing this outstanding indebtedness. The example thus ignores the other operating costs which the lessor might incur. Account is however taken of the lessor's need to establish and maintain a doubtful debt provision—the amount of this being set at 1% of the figure at which the asset is stated in the lessor's balance sheet. After the lessor has repaid his borrowings, he invests all surplus cash to yield 2½% per quarter.

Taxation, as has been mentioned earlier, is a significant factor contributing to the growth of leasing, and the benefits it offers. However the principles we are seeking to illustrate and clarify in this section can be very well demonstrated without taking tax into account. Tax, and how it alters the picture, will be dealt with from paragraph 2.61 onwards.

THE CASH FLOW FORECAST

2.08 The data in the preceeding paragraph can be turned into a cash flow forecast as follows:-

		Rent receivable before beginning of quarter	Outstanding borrowing at beginning of quarter	Interest payable at end of quarter	Outstanding borrowing at end of quarter
Year 1	Q1	£(7,100)	£92,900	£ 3,251	£96,151
	Q2	(7,100)	89,051	3,117	92,168
	Q3	(7,100)	85,068	2,977	88,045
	Q4	(7,100)	80,945	2,833	83,778
				£12,178	
Year 2	Q1	(7,100)	76,678	2,684	79,362
	Q2	(7,100)	72,262	2,529	74,791
	Q3	(7,100)	67,691	2,369	70,060
	Q4	(7,100)	62,960	2,204	65,164
				£ 9,786	
Year 3	Q1	(7,100)	58,064	2,032	60,096
	Q2	(7,100)	52,996	1,855	54,851
	Q3	(7,100)	47,751	1,671	49,422
	Q4	(7,100)	42,322	1,481	43,803
				£ 7,039	
Year 4	Q1	(7,100)	36,703	1,285	37,988
	Q2	(7,100)	30,888	1,081	31,969
	Q3	(7,100)	24,869	870	25,739
	Q4	(7,100)	18,639	652	19,291
				£ 3,888	
Year 5	Q1	(7,100)	12,191	427	12,618
	Q2	(7,100)	5,518	193	5,711
				£ 620	
	Q3	(7,100)	(1,389)	(35)	(1,424)
	Q4	(7,100)	(8,524)	(213)	(8,737)
				£(248)	

THE STRAIGHT-LINE METHOD

2.09 The asset owned by the lessor company is depreciated on a straight-line basis over the lease period. The profit and loss account figures, and the balance sheet amounts at which the asset is stated, are arrived at as follows:-

Profit & Loss	Year 1	Year 2	Year 3	Year 4	Year 5	Total
Rent	£28,400	£28,400	£28,400	£28,400	£28,400	£142,000
Depreciation	(20,000)	(20,000)	(20,000)	(20,000)	(20,000)	(100,000)
	8,400	8,400	8,400	8,400	8,400	42,000
Interest	(12,178)	(9,786)	(7,039)	(3,888)	(372)	(33,263)
	(3,778)	(1,386)	1,361	4,512	8,028	8,737
Doubtful Debts	(800)	200	200	200	200	–
Profit (Loss)	£ (4,578)	£ (1,186)	£ 1,561	£ 4,712	£ 8,228	£ 8,737

Balance Sheet at year end					
Asset amount	£80,000	£60,000	£40,000	£20,000	–
Outstanding borrowing	83,778	65,164	43,803	19,291	(8,737)
Doubtful debts provision	800	600	400	200	–
Cumulative profit (loss) to date	(4,578)	(5,764)	(4,203)	509	8,737
	80,000	60,000	40,000	20,000	

DOUBTFUL DEBT PROVISIONS

2.10 First, it would be helpful to deal with one small point concerning the preparation of these figures, and those shown in each of the following examples. The line described as doubtful debts is the amount put to provision for doubtful debts, or released from that provision. The amount of that provision is maintained for illustration purposes at 1% of the figure at which the asset is stated in each year's balance sheet. At the end of the first year, after depreciation of £20,000, the asset stands in the balance sheet at £80,000. Doubtful debts provision of £800 is therefore created, by debiting this amount to profit and loss account.

In the second years accounts, with the asset standing at £60,000, it is possible to release £200 from the doubtful debts provision reducing its balance from £800 to £600.

In the examples which follow, depreciation is the major variable. It is the formula by which the profit and loss account charge for depreciation is fixed that primarily determines the pattern of profits and losses between years. However, the doubtful debts provision varies in sympathy. The amounts put to that provision or released from it therefore differ in each example.

2.11 Reverting to the straight line example in paragraph 209, it is difficult to believe that the "bottom line" losses and profits are particularly meaningful. As we have already pointed out in paragraph 2.06 the greater activity and risk in the early years of the lease should be reflected by a greater allocation of profits in those years.

RE-EXAMINATION OF FINANCIAL ASSUMPTIONS

2.12 This distortion in the profit flow is primarily caused by three financial assumptions. First, we have assumed that the lessor finances his transaction entirely with borrowed funds. In the balance sheet of a leasing subsidiary of a major bank, this may be an approximation to the truth. It can never be wholly true, simultaneously, for all of a company's current leases. An independent company would perhaps be unlikely to be able to support borrowings in excess of four times the amount of its shareholders funds. Even in the case of the subsidiary of the bank the depositors, (whose funds enable the bank to onlend to its subsidiary), only put their funds into the bank on the strength of its capital position so that on a "group" basis finance cannot be regarded as wholly borrowed.

2.13 Secondly we have assumed that all cash not used in paying interest is promptly used to reduce borrowings. This is never true; expenses must absorb some, and so also must dividends and retentions to maintain shareholders funds against inflation, or to expand them.

2.14 Each of these two assumptions has an effect on the amount of the interest charge in each of the five years of the lease period. In practice, if a smaller proportion of the necessary funds had to be borrowed from external sources, and if the repayment of those borrowings were not accomplished so quickly and singlemindedly as we have assumed, then the interest charge in the early years would probably be smaller, and in the later years as high or higher, than in our illustration. If this were the position the "slope" of the profit line would be less marked; the early years losses would be smaller, and the later years profits would also be less.

2.15 The third financial assumption is of a different kind. If a leasing company has at all material times twenty identical items of plant out on hire, these leases having been entered into at quarterly intervals, then its aggregate borrowings could well remain constant. It will in fact be generating a positive cash flow of £34,948 per annum, (8,737 x 20 ÷ 5), and to this extent it could, (but need not), reduce its indebtedness.

2.16 It is clear, however, that whether or not the company makes the assumption that particular parts of the indebtedness are allocable to specific leases, the aggregate interest charge remains constant. Secondly, and this is a separate point, aggregate profit similarly stands unaltered. This is because the determinant of the profit from any lease in any year is the depreciation of the relevant asset. With twenty assets of exactly evenly spaced ages, the company can use any depreciation policy it likes, so long as it is consistent in its use of it, without affecting its aggregate profit levels.

2.17 So what merit is there in examining accounting methods on an individual lease by lease method to determine the truth and fairness of the results reflected for each transaction in each year? The answer must surely be that it is the only possible way in which one can proceed. One cannot assume an even flow of business, of identical characteristics, past and future. One cannot therefore rely on the evenhandedness of swings and roundabouts. The only possible accounting technique is to ensure that each lease is accounted for on a sound basis. Only thus can the aggregate of all of those results be trusted.

2.18 This approach is the justification for all three of our financial assumptions, not just for the last of them. It is not to say that the particular assumptions built into our example are uniquely right; it might well be sensible to build into the figures not only some allowance for expenses but also a recognition of dividend requirements and of retentions on that part of the lease finance provided out of shareholders funds rather than by borrowings. But what one can say is that the absence of these does not invalidate the approach we have used.

219 If the approach is reasonable, are the results also reasonable? Here the answer must be that they are open to serious criticism. As already indicated, if a lease can be expected to be profitable overall, then one might expect a significant amount of that profit to be recognised early in the period. The straight-line method not only fails to produce this answer, but gives losses in the first two years which are only made good in the third and fourth. Cumulatively, practically the whole profit is located in the final year.

THE MARKET VALUE METHOD

2.20 The distinguishing feature of the next method, known as the market value method, is that depreciation is charged on a basis consistent with the asset's being shown in each year's balance sheet at an amount no greater than might be received if it were to be sold.

Profit & Loss	Year 1	Year 2	Year 3	Year 4	Year 5	Total
Rent	£28,400	£28,400	£28,400	£28,400	£28,400	£142,000
Depreciation	(40,000)	(25,000)	(15,000)	(10,000)	(10,000)	(100,000)
	(11,600)	3,400	13,400	18,400	18,400	42,000
Interest	(12,178)	(9,786)	(7,039)	(3,888)	(372)	(33,263)
	(23,778)	(6,386)	6,361	14,512	18,028	8,737
Doubtful Debts	(600)	250	150	100	100	–
Profit (Loss)	£(24,378)	£ (6,136)	£ 6,511	£14,612	£18,128	£ 8,737
Balance Sheet at year end						
Asset Amount	£60,000	£35,000	£20,000	£10,000	–	

2.21 Little comment is needed on this method. If the straight-line method is open to criticism, every one of those criticisms applies with increased force to the market value method.

THE DEFENCE OF STRAIGHT-LINE AND MARKET VALUE METHODS

2.22 In paragraphs 2.19 and 2.21 we have condemned each of the two accounting methods examined for failing to measure up against certain preconceived and theoretical notions of the way in which profit is generated. What arguments are advanced in their favour?

RECOGNISING PROFITS LATER RATHER THAN SOONER

2.23 There are three good pragmatic reasons for recognising profits later rather than earlier. First, there is tax. This is encapsulated in Lord Reid's judgment in the BSC Footwear case, (47 TC at page 524), "it is well settled that the ordinary principles of commercial accounting must be used except in so far as any specific statutory provision requires otherwise". Undoubtedly the straight-line and market value methods could each be described as ordinary commercial accounting at the time Lord Reid was speaking. They can still be so described today. Once an accounting standard has been issued, and has come into force, that position would in our view no longer hold true. Meanwhile, if the judiciary has given the accountancy profession some latitude, why frame your accounts in such a way as to advance the due date of payment of tax?

(Note that the accelerated capital allowances for investment in plant and machinery may to some extent mask the effects of recognition of profits earlier or later. Given sufficient taxable income in the company or in the group to absorb these capital allowances, it is only a masking effect and not a change in the underlying disadvantage of bringing income into the tax charge earlier than necessary).

2.24 The second good pragmatic reason is that in a period of high sustained inflation, the historic cost convention not only overstates profits, but makes it more difficult for businesses, and even more so their shareholders, to perceive the level of retention needed to preserve capital capacity. (As we will see later, stock appreciation relief for tax purposes does not apply to leased assets). It is therefore said to be sensible to err on the side of understating profits rather than on the other side. This erring is described as being "prudent", although the extent of some of this prudence suggests that erring would be better described as being in error.

2.25 Thirdly, and not unrelated to the other two, one must never try to understand a business without regard to the context and constraints in which it operates and against which its management ethos has been created. Two particular points are relevant here. First, in the late 1950's there was a crisis in the hire purchase finance industry, as a result of which a number of finance companies very nearly went to the wall. Comment at the time focussed on unsound accounting practices which misled management about the true state of business to such an extent that a downturn in economic activity caught the companies concerned substantially unawares. Whether or not that is a true analysis of what happened matters less than whether the current management of leasing companies think it is a true analysis.

2.26 A related point to be borne in mind is the close links between banking and leasing both in terms of ownership of a significant part of the leasing industry by the banks, and in terms of interchangeability of personnel. There are even perhaps bankers brought up under the non-disclosure provisions of Part III of the 8th Schedule to the 1948 Companies Act who might be suspected of believing that the full disclosure imposed on non-banking companies, (and now voluntarily accepted by many banks), still entitles them to carry in "inner reserves" what most other people would regard as disclosable and distributable profits. It is easy to overstate the importance of this factor, but it is equally unwise to pretend that it does not exist.

THE ARGUMENT AGAINST THE STRAIGHT-LINE AND MARKET VALUE METHODS

2.27 Tax, inflation and unhappy memories are three good reasons why recognition of profits should be delayed as long as possible. The counter-argument is as follows.

The lessor is in what is basically a financial business. The money he has borrowed, and is repaying in stages, is being used to generate a financial return. Although he has used his borrowing to acquire an asset, and it is that asset rather than money which he has "lent". it is analogous to a loan of money in that each amount of rent he receives from the lessee can be recognised as containing an element representing interest, and another the return of capital.

2.28 How much interest, and how much capital is the $64,000 question. Consider the following table:-

		Repaid to provider of loan capital		Received from Lessee	
		Interest	**Capital**	**Analogous to interest**	**Analogous to capital**
Year 1		£12,178	£16,222	£12,178	£16,222
Year 2		9,786	18,614	9,786	18,614
Year 3		7,039	21,361	7,039	21,361
Year 4		3,888	24,512	3,888	24,512
Year 5	Q1	427	6,673	427	6,673
	Q2	193	6,907	193	6,907
	Q3	–	5,711	35	7,100
	Q4	–	–	213	7,100
		33,511	100,000	33,759	108,489
			33,511		33,759
			133,511		142,248
					133,511
				Ending net profit	£ 8,737

The left hand two columns are the relationship of the lessor with the provider of his loan capital.

The right hand two columns, for the first six lines, are no more than an arbitrary split of the rent receipts. On the seventh and eigth lines are the two items of interest received and the final rental receipts.

2.29 What guidance can we get from this table? The first six lines, and a part of the figure on the seventh line of the extreme right hand column, that part of the rent receipts comparable to the capital repayments, are also analogous to a depreciation charge. That means that the interest part of the rent receipt, is "matched" in the profit and loss account with the charge for interest paid. If we ignore for a moment the advisability of some provision for doubtful debts, the profit and loss account in each of the first four-and-a-half years will show neither profit nor loss.

MATCHING OF INCOME AND EXPENSE

2.30 The matching of income and expense is a fundamental accounting principle, but is that what matching means?

The figures set out in the table are neither more nor less than cash flow accounting. They show income being credited to match expense, rather than expense being debited against the appropriate income. Unless we are dealing with a cash business, it is incorrect to believe that no profit should be recognized until all capital invested has been repaid to the original investor i.e. that the £8,737 left in the hands of the lessor at the end of the fifth year can be said to have arisen as profit like this:

Year 5	30 June	–	part of rent receipt	£1,389
	30 September	–	interest on investment of above	35
		–	final rent receipt	7,100
	31 December	–	interest on investment of above	213
				£8,737

2.31 Matching of income and expenditure implies a re-timing of one or other. Usually it involves carrying forward expenditure from the period in which it was incurred, so that it is debited in the profit and loss account of the later period in which the income generated by that expense is received.

In full payout leasing the matching of income and expense proceeds from the same concepts and principles, but its application is not so straightforward.

2.32 Why it can be more difficult can best be demonstrated if we use the analogy of a trader who purchases a machine for himself. His income from operating that machine is the gross margin he makes on selling the additional goods produced on the machine. This margin can perhaps be expected to be level initially when the machine is new and efficient. As the machine gets older, and relatively less efficient through wear and tear or obsolescence, it may well be that the amount of income will fall.

On the other side of our trader's profit and loss account there will appear the interest on his borrowings for the machine and the depreciation. There will also be amounts of expense on repairs and maintenance of the machine—these last amounts being low initially and rising as the machine gets older. The trader's net profit from the machine is the difference between the income it generates and the expense associated with it. If this net profit is anticipated to be relatively level throughout the machine's life, then the trader will not think it appropriate to "retime" any of his expenditure—he already has an acceptable matching of it against income. Similarly if net profit increases gently through the machine's life such a pattern can be defended as being a true and fair view of reality.

2.33 Let us, however, revert to the lessor. He has completely level rental receipts and has sharply declining expenses (comprising interest and depreciation but not repairs and maintenance). We have seen initial year's losses, and high levels of profit thereafter in both the straight-line and market value methods.

Correspondingly the lessee who takes the machine on lease will inevitably show a different pattern of profits over the years from what would have resulted had he purchased instead of leasing. We will look at this side of the coin in due course in chapter 4—whether the lessee should report higher profits in the early years. His rental expenses would then be less than the aggregate of interest and depreciation. This is not an easy question, and we cannot settle it here.

What we can say is that it is unreasonable that the financier who assists that lessee by making available the asset, should himself take into his own profit and loss account in the early years the whole of what we might describe as the adverse expense levels of those early years. But how is he to decide how much of the expense it would be appropriate to match against his rental income in each of those early years?

2.34 This is the fundamental difficulty of matching the expenditure of lessors against their rental income. It is a difficulty which the straight-line and the market value methods do not really face up to. Indeed the market value method, in particular, produced in paragraph 2.20 a result which so signally failed to make any match, that we can perhaps drop this method from further consideration. It is easier to do so because the market value method is not commonly used, nor does it carry any wide acceptance.

On the other hand the remaining three accounting methods, the annuity, rule of 78 and investment period methods, do attempt to resolve the matching problem. We now turn to an examination of each of them.

THE ANNUITY METHOD

2.35 The concept underlying this method is the idea already mentioned in paragraph 2.27 that each year's rent receipt can be regarded as analogous to an annuity receipt—comprising an element representing return of capital, and an element representing interest on the amount of capital outstanding.

2.36 An annuity of £28,400 for five years, purchased at a cost of £100,000, yields the grantor a rate of 12.955% the figures being as follows:-

	Year 1	Year 2	Year 3	Year 4	Year 5
Capital outstanding at beginning	£100,000	£84,555	£67,109	£47,403	£25,144
Interest thereon	12,955	10,954	8,694	6,141	3,256
Balance of annual instalment is capital repaid	15,445	17,446	19,706	22,259	25,144
Capital outstanding at year end	£ 84,555	£67,109	£47,403	£25,144	–

2.37 The profit and loss account and the balance sheet amounts at which the asset is stated are derived from this annuity calculation:-

Profit & Loss	Year 1	Year 2	Year 3	Year 4	Year 5	Total
Rent	£28,400	£28,400	£28,400	£28,400	£28,400	£142,000
Depreciation	(15,445)	(17,446)	(19,706)	(22,259)	(25,144)	(100,000)
	12,955	10,954	8,694	6,141	3,256	42,000
Interest	(12,178)	(9,786)	(7,039)	(3,888)	(372)	(33,263)
	777	1,168	1,655	2,253	2,884	8,737
Doubtful Debts	(846)	175	197	223	251	–
Profit (Loss)	(69)	1,343	1,852	2,476	3,135	8,737
Balance Sheet at year end						
Asset Amount	£84,555	£67,109	£47,403	£25,144	–	

2.38 It is of course implicit from the above that the profit before expenses in each year shows a constant yield of 12.955% on the "capital unrecovered" at the previous year end. £10,954 for instance is 12.955% of £84,555, and so is £8,694 of £67,109.

RECALCULATION ON QUARTERLY RESTS

2.39 Using quarterly rests in place of annual, the effective rate is exactly 3.6% per quarter, (15.196% per annum), and the "annuity" is as follows:

		Capital Outstanding	Interest	Quarterly Payments Capital	Total
Year 1	Q1	100,000	3,600	3,500	7,100
	Q2	96,500	3,474	3,626	7,100
	Q3	92,874	3,343	3,757	7,100
	Q4	89,117	3,208	3,892	7,100
				14,775	
Year 2	Q1	85,225	3,068	4,032	7,100
	Q2	81,193	2,923	4,177	7,100
	Q3	77,016	2,773	4,327	7,100
	Q4	72,689	2,617	4,483	7,100
				17,019	
Year 3	Q1	68,206	2,455	4,645	7,100
	Q2	63,561	2,288	4,812	7,100
	Q3	58,749	2,115	4,985	7,100
	Q4	53,764	1,936	5,164	7,100
				19,606	
Year 4	Q1	48,600	1,750	5,350	7,100
	Q2	43,250	1,557	5,543	7,100
	Q3	37,707	1,358	5,742	7,100
	Q4	31,965	1,151	5,949	7,100
				22,584	
Year 5	Q1	26,016	937	6,163	7,100
	Q2	19,853	715	6,385	7,100
	Q3	13,468	485	6,615	7,100
	Q4	6,853	247	6,853	7,100
				26,016	
			42,000	100,000	

2.40 Translating these figures into a profit and loss account for the lease produces the following set of figures:-

	Year 1	Year 2	Year 3	Year 4	Year 5	Total
Rental	28,400	28,400	28,400	28,400	28,400	142,000
Depreciation	(14,775)	(17,019)	(19,606)	(22,584)	(26,016)	(100,000)
	13,625	11,381	8,794	5,816	2,384	42,000
Interest	(12,178)	(9,786)	(7,039)	(3,888)	(372)	(33,263)
	1,447	1,595	1,755	1,928	2,012	8,737
Doubtful Debts	(852)	170	196	226	260	–
	595	1,765	1,951	2,154	2,272	8,737
Amount at which asset stated at year end	85,225	68,206	48,600	26,016	–	

OPTICAL ILLUSION

2.41 It is perhaps worth looking at the question how a leasing company can borrow money at 3½% per quarter, equivalent to 14.75% per annum, and make a profit as large as £8,737 out of using reducing amounts of it through the lease period in a way which yields 3.6%, equivalent to 15.196% per annum. This is an optical illusion.

The funds borrowed were effectively £92,900 not £100,000, because the first quarter's rent received at the commencement of that quarter immediately reduced the amount outstanding. This acceleration is a continuing feature through the lease period.

THE £92,900 ANNUITY

2.42 The key to a proper understanding and application of the annuity method is this fact. We should not be looking for an annuity calculation which repays £100,000 by means of 20 instalmentsof £7,100, but one which repays £92,900 by means of 19 instalments. This is tabulated below.

2.43 An annuity to repay £92,900 by means of 19 quarterly payments of £7,100, using quarterly rests, would give a quarterly interest rate of 4.045%, equivalent to 17.19% per annum.

		Capital Outstanding	Interest	Quarterly Payments Capital	Total
Year 1	Q1	£92,900	£ 3,758	£ 3,342	£7,100
	Q2	89,558	3,623	3,477	7,100
	Q3	86,081	3,480	3,620	7,100
	Q4	82,461	3,335	3,765	7,100
				£14,204	
Year 2	Q1	78,696	3,183	3,917	7,100
	Q2	74,779	3,025	4.075	7,100
	Q3	70,704	2,859	4,241	7,100
	Q4	66,463	2,688	4,412	7,100
				£16,645	
Year 3	Q1	62,051	2,510	4,590	7,100
	Q2	57,461	2,325	4,775	7,100
	Q3	52,686	2,130	4,970	7,100
	Q4	47,716	1,929	5,171	7,100
				£19,506	
Year 4	Q1	42,545	1,721	5,379	7,100
	Q2	37,166	1,504	5,596	7,100
	Q3	31,570	1,276	5,824	7,100
	Q4	25,746	1,041	6,059	7,100
				£22,858	
Year 5	Q1	£19,687	£ 797	£ 6,303	7,100
	Q2	13,384	541	6,559	7,100
	Q3	6,825	275	6,825	7,100
	Q4	–	–	–	–
				£19,687	
			£42,000	£92,900	

2.44 The resulting profit and loss account is as follows:

	Year 1	Year 2	Year 3	Year 4	Year 5	Total
Rent	£28,400	£18,400	£28,400	£28,400	£28,400	£142,000
Depreciation	(14,204)	(16,645)	(19,506)	(22,858)	(26,787)	(100,000)
	£14,196	£11,755	£ 8,894	£ 5,542	£ 1,613	£ 42,000
Interest	(12,178)	(9,786)	(7,039)	(3,888)	(372)	(33,263)
	£ 2,018	£ 1,969	£ 1,855	£ 1,654	£ 1,241	£ 8,737
Doubtful Debts	(858)	166	195	229	268	–
	£ 1,160	£ 2,135	£ 2,050	£ 1,883	£ 1,509	£ 8,737
Balance sheet at end of year						
Asset amount	£85,796	£69,151	£49,645	£26,787	–	

VALIDITY OF THE ANNUITY METHOD

2.45 The annuity method has conceptual validity. Since the rent is equivalent to the total instalment of the annuity, and depreciation to the capital element of it, it follows that the first subtotal line in the profit and loss account is equivalent to the interest element of the annuity. In fact the interest in the first four quarters in the paragraph 2.39 calculation is £13,625, and in the equivalent quarters in paragraph 2.43 is £14,196. These figures show up in the relevant profit and loss accounts in paragraphs 2.40 and 2.44 respectively.

However, matching this interest element in the notional annuity receipt with the actual interest paid, gives the following pattern, (taken from the level of the next subtotal in the profit and loss accounts).

	Year 1	Year 2	Year 3	Year 4	Year 5	Total
"£100,000 Annuity"	£1,447	£1,595	£1,755	£1,928	£2,012	£8,737
"£92,900 Annuity"	£2,018	£1,969	£1,855	£1,654	£1,241	£8,737

The upward and the downward trend cannot both be correct. The authors hope that they have satisfactorily explained in paragraph 2.42 that the second of the two is based on sound logic whereas the first is not. It will not have escaped the reader's notice that the authors' prejudices lie in favour of the downward sloping line.

2.46 Our experience suggests the "£92,900 Annuity" method is not the form met most often in lessor's accounts. The more straightforward but cruder "£100,000", calculation seems to be understood by a a larger number of people, and therefore recognised as being "right" despite its obvious fallacy. However we will continue to use the £92,000 rather than the £100,000 method in all further examples, because it gives a more logical and acceptable result.

THE RULE OF 78, (OR SUM OF THE DIGITS) METHOD

2.47 There are two variants of this method. Both achieve an apportionment of income in the ratio of one part to the final period of the lease, two parts to the penultimate period, three parts to the period before that, and so on. In a five year lease with rent payable annually, the income would be apportioned 5:4:3:2:1 into the five years. If the rent were payable quarterly the proportions would be 74:58:42:26:10. The first of these figures is 20+19+18+17, the second is 16+15+14+13, and the last is 4+3+2+1.
(The rule of 78 derives its name from the sum of the numbers from 1 to 12 inclusive).

THE "STRAIGHT" RULE

2.48 Under the "Straight" rule of 78, the lessor depreciates his asset in accordance with the formula. He also recognises profit in the same manner. Doing these simultaneously can only be achieved if a debtor is created and shown in the balance sheet in the early years of the lease, in respect of rent not yet receivable but for which credit is taken in measuring profit. The various relationships are very easy to see if we use 5:4:3:2:1 proportions; the figures appear as follows:

	Year 1	Year 2	Year 3	Year 4	Year 5	Total
Rent	£28,400	£28,400	£28,400	£28,400	£28,400	£142,000
Depreciation (5:4:3:2:1)	(33,333)	(26,667)	(20,000)	(13,333)	(6,667)	(100,000)
	(4,933)	1,733	8,400	15,067	21,733	42,000
Debtor	18,933	9,467	–	(9,467)	(18,933)	–
(5:4:3:2:1)	14,000	11,200	8,400	5,600	2,800	42,000
Interest	(12,178)	(9,786)	(7,039)	(3,888)	(372)	(33,263)
	1,822	1,414	1,361	1,712	2,428	8,737
Doubtful Debts	(856)	172	200	228	256	–
	£ 966	£ 1,586	£ 1,561	£ 1,940	£ 2,684	£ 8,737
Balance Sheet at end of year						
Asset Amount	66,667	40,000	20,000	6,667	–	
Debtor	18,933	28,400	28,400	18,933	–	
	£85,600	£68,400	£48,400	£25,600	–	

THE "REVERSE" RULE

2.49 In the second variant, the so called "Reverse" rule of 78, the same position is achieved in the profit and loss account without crediting in the account amounts of rent not yet due. This is done by designing the depreciation charge to achieve the income flow which is required. The figures appear as below. It will be seen that the balance sheet figures at which the leased asset is stated are the same as the aggregates in the "straight" case of the asset amounts and the debtor amounts.

	Year 1	Year 2	Year 3	Year 4	Year 5	Total
Rent	£28,400	£28,400	£28,400	£28,400	£28,400	£142,000
Depreciation	(14,400)	(17,200)	(20,000)	(22,800)	(25,600)	(100,000)
	14,000	11,200	8,400	5,600	2,800	42,000
	....	....	.... then	as before	....	....
	£ 966	£ 1,586	£ 1,561	£ 1,940	£ 2,684	£ 8,737
Balance sheet at end of year						
Asset Amount	£85,600	£68,400	£48,400	£25,600	–	

The reverse rule of 78 is the more commonly met of the two. So much so that for all practical purposes we can ignore the "straight" rule in all our workings from here on, and we can conform to the normal terminology by referring simply to the rule of 78 without specifying whether it is the straight or the reverse application of the rule. In comparison to the depreciation charges in the straight-line and market value methods, the line showing depreciation in each of the five years in the above example looks odd. We have seen in the annuity method, and shall see when we come to the remaining accounting method, the investment period, that it is not all that dissimilar from their depreciation charges. But the final line, profit after depreciation, interest and doubtful debts, appears to be rather more defensible than were the equivalent lines in the straightline and market value.

QUARTERLY RESTS

2.50 Applying the rule of 78 on the basis of quarterly rests, that is assuming rent receipts of £7,100 per quarter rather than £28,400 per annum, produces the marginally different pattern set out below:-

	Year 1	Year 2	Year 3	Year 4	Year 5	Total
Rent	£28,400	£28,400	£28,400	£28,400	£28,400	£142,000
Depreciation	(13,600)	(16,800)	(20,000)	(23,200)	(26,400)	(100,000)
	14,800	11,600	8,400	5,200	2,000	42,000
Interest	(12,178)	(9,786)	(7,039)	(3,888)	(372)	(33,263)
	2,622	1,814	1,361	1,312	1,628	8,737
Doubtful Debts	(864)	168	200	232	264	—
	£ 1,758	£ 1,982	£ 1,561	£ 1,544	£ 1,892	£ 8,737
Balance Sheet at end of year						
Asset Amount	£86,400	£69,600	£49,600	£26,400	—	

WHEN THE RESULTS MAY BE INVALID

2.51 One of the great virtues of the rule of 78 is its relative simplicity. However in three respects this method has drawbacks. First, the rule of 78 tends to produce figures which are not completely acceptable if the lease is for more than about ten years, and/or if the rate of interest implicit in the lease is greater than about 15%. Its shortcomings in this respect result from its being a simple formula which is not capable of producing a completely accurate answer in the whole range of possible cases. Secondly, the figures produced may be reasonable where rents are level throughout the lease, and where the investment in the lease decreases relatively evenly. When either or both of these conditions are not met, the principles underlying the 78's method are incapable of adjustment to produce figures which are not distorted by the asymmetry of rents or indebtedness. Step rents and balloon rents, dealt with in paragraph 3.96 et seq below, will thus not give a reasonable profit profile under the rule of 78. Thirdly, tax based leases, examined in paragraphs 2.70 et seq below, are subject to significant distortions if accounted for by 78's.

2.52 The differences between the figures on an annual rent basis, and on quarterly rests, are a warning about the degree of care needed in using this method, (and the next one, for that matter).

	Year 1	Year 2	Year 3	Year 4	Year 5	Total
Sum of quarterly digits (paragraph 2.50)	£2,622	£1,814	£1,361	£1,312	£1,628	£8,737
Sum of annual digits (paragraph 2.48)	1,822	1,414	1,361	1,712	2,428	8,737

An extra £800 of profit into the first year and £400 into the second is a large movement compared to the total level of profits, and makes a completely different slope in the post-interest, pre-doubtful debt, profit line. Commonsense tells us that the figures calculated on quarterly rests are likely to be less arbitrary than those on an annual basis. Observation of the result appears to bear this out. It shows a trend of profits which is a nearer approximation to the pattern which we have argued to be logical, true and fair.

If we were to recalculate once more, this time on a sum of the monthly digits, (rather than on a quarterly basis), the apportionment of gross income between years would be in the ratio 654 : 510 : 366 : 222 : 78, the sum of these being 1,830 which is the sum of the digits in a sixty month period. The post-interest, pre-doubtful debt, line would be:-

	Year 1	Year 2	Year 3	Year 4	Year 5	Total
Sum of monthly digits	£2,832	£1,919	£1,361	£1,207	£1,418	£8,737
Sum of quarterly digits (paragraph 2.50)	2,622	1,814	1,361	1,312	1,628	8,737

This "monthly" calculation appears to produce an even better result, judged against the same criteria of what is thought to be true and fair.

INVESTMENT PERIOD METHOD

2.53 The last of the five methods of accounting is regarded by its devotees as the most sophisticated and logically satisfying.

It is based, first, on the identification of each lease's investment period, that is the period up to the date at which the borrowings are finally and permanently repaid. Then, the lease income is apportioned through that period by reference to the outstanding borrowings at each point.

2.54 On yearly rests, the cash invested in our lease can be read off the cash flow statement as follows.
The income is apportioned in the same ratio:-

			Gross income apportioned
Cash invested end of year	**1**	£83,778	£16,595
	2	65,164	12,908
	3	43,803	8,676
	4	19,291	3,821
	5	(Positive)	–
		£212,036	£42,000

For year 1, as an example, this apportionment is by reference to the formula:

$$\frac{83,778}{212,036} \times 42,000$$

2.55 The profit and loss account and balance sheet asset amounts are therefore as follows:-

	Year 1	Year 2	Year 3	Year 4	Year 5	Total
Rent	£28,400	£28,400	£28,400	£28,400	£28,400	£142,000
Depreciation	(11,805)	(15,492)	(19,724)	(24,579)	(28,400)	(100,000)
	16,595	12,908	8,676	3,821	–	42,000
Interest	(12,178)	(9,786)	(7.039)	(3,888)	(372)	(33,263)
	4,417	3,122	1,637	(67)	(372)	8,737
Doubtful Debts	(882)	155	197	246	284	–
	£ 3,535	£ 3,277	£ 1,834	£ 179	£(88)	£ 8,737

Balance Sheet at end of year					
Asset Amount	£88,195	£72,703	£52,979	£28,400	–

QUARTERLY RESTS

2.56 Once again, analysing the cash flow on quarterly rests gives a more precise picture. The investment period lasts from the first quarter of year 1 to the second quarter of year 5. The outstanding borrowings at each of these quarterly rests can be seen to be as follows:-

Year 1	1st Quarter	£96,151)		(4 Quarters of	
	2nd Quarter	92,168)	Giving	(Year 1	£15,262
	3rd Quarter	88,045)	Apportionment	(Year 2	12,264
	.. and so on to ..	)	of income	(Year 3	8,823
Year 4	4th Quarter	19,291)		(Year 4	4,874
Year 5	1st Quarter	12,618)		(Year 5	777
	2nd Quarter	5,711)			
		£991,007			£42,000

2.57 On this basis the profit and loss account and balance sheet amounts are:-

	Year 1	Year 2	Year 3	Year 4	Year 5	Total
Rent	£28,400	£28,400	£28,400	£28,400	£28,400	£142,000
Depreciation	(13,138)	(16,136)	(19,577)	(23,526)	(27,623)	(100,000)
	15,262	12,264	8,823	4,874	777	42,000
Interest	(12,178)	(9,786)	(7,039)	(3,888)	(372)	(33,263)
	3,084	2,478	1,784	986	405	8,737
Doubtful Debts	(869)	162	196	235	276	–
	2,215	2,640	1,980	1,221	681	8,737
Balance Sheet at end of year						
Asset Amount	£86,862	£70,726	£51,149	£27,623	–	

2.58 The system is more sophisticated than the rule of 78. This means not only that it can be argued with greater force that it has a sound theoretical basis, and that it will produce a closer approximation to truth over a wider range of circumstances. It means also that it is much more complex to operate.

DETERMINATION OF THE INVESTMENT PERIOD

2.59 The first of those complexities is the determination of the investment period. In our figures the whole of the profit generated has been utilised in repayment of the borrowing. This is sometimes referred to as the profits being reinvested in the lease. The alternative way of constructing a cash flow statement for our particular lease would be to show part or all of those profits being withdrawn from it for application elsewhere in the leasing company. The investment period could be materially lengthened as a result. The length of the investment period could also be affected by changes during the lease period in the data on which the original cash flows had been forecast. But whether the figures should or should not be recalculated is a question to which we shall return below.

2.60 The calculations are complex and may need recalculation e.g. if currencies other than sterling are involved. But a particular advantage is that the initial calculations themselves are an excellent method of judging the likely profitability of proposed business.

ADDING THE TAX CHARGE INTO THE ACCOUNTS

2.61 Tax figures can now be added onto the figures we have developed above for the purposes of the profit and loss account. Taking those prepared on the rule of 78 basis, (paragraph 2.50) the computations look like this:-

	Year 1	Year 2	Year 3	Year 4	Year 5
Profit per accounts	£ 1,758	£ 1,982	£ 1,561	£ 1,544	£ 1,892
Disallow Depreciation	13,600	16,800	20,000	23,200	26,400
Doubtful Debts	864	(168)	(200)	(232)	(264)
	16,222	18,614	21,361	24,512	28,028
Capital Allowances	(100,000)	–	–	–	–
	(83,778)	18,614	21,361	24,512	28,028
Loss b/fwd	–	(83,778)	(65,164)	(43,803)	(19,291)
Loss c/fwd	(83,778)	(65,164)	(43,803)	(19,291)	–
Profit	–	–	–	–	£ 8,737

THE STRAIGHTFORWARD COMPUTATION

2.62 The foregoing is the computation as prepared for the taxman. A more straightforward way would be to prepare the figures in this manner.

	Year 1	Year 2	Year 3	Year 4	Year 5
Rent	£28,400	£28,400	£28,400	£28,400	£28,400
Capital Allowance	(100,000)				
Interest Paid	(12,178)	(9,786)	(7,039)	(3,888)	(620)
Interest Received					248
	£(83,778)	18,614	21,361	24,512	28,028
Loss b/fwd	–	(83,778)	(65,164)	(43,803)	(19,291)
Loss c/fwd	(83,778)	(65,164)	(43,803)	(19,291)	–
Profit	–	–	–	–	£ 8,737

2.63 From this second computation it will be apparent that the final results for tax purposes are going to be the same whatever method of accounting is used. The dictum of Lord Reid quoted in paragraph 2.23 above that profits for tax should be computed on normal principles of commercial accountancy is wholly irrelevant here. We made out that recognising profits as late as possible would similarly defer tax liabilities. It does not, and the reason why it does not is an illustration how carefully we need to examine each of our propositions, even those which appear to be completely self evident.

2.64 The profits generated by this lease and assessable to tax amount to £8,737, and whatever accounting method is adopted, that assessment will be raised for year 5. At 52% the liability would be £4,543, and would be due for payment on 1 October in year 6, (or later if the company had preserved from pre-1965 a longer tax payment interval).

DEFERRED TAXATION

2.65 But the company would also need to consider whether it could properly account without providing in full for deferred taxation. A leasing company will normally be unable to justify not providing, for the following reasons:-

a) its cont[illegible]d ability in the future to write the same volume of leasing [illegible]iness may be dependent upon the continued availabi[illegible] of capital allowances at the current 100% rate:

b) similar[illegible]he volume of future business written depends in most case[illegible] upon the ability of other companies in the group to absorb the losses created in the leasing companies' tax computations by those 100% capital allowances. It may be that the "taxable capacity" of the other group companies will shrink. Alternatively, those companies may find other, more profitable, ways of eliminating their tax liabilities.

The company must provide for deferred tax unless it can demonstrate that the tax concerned will not become payable in the foreseeable future. Our view is that the uncertainties in (a) and (b) above mean that the company is unlikely to be able to demonstrate this. Let us assume therefore that provision is to be made, and consider what is necessary. The figures which we have been looking at, those derived in paragraph 2.50 from the rule of 78 method, using quarterly rests, were as follows:-

	Year 1	Year 2	Year 3	Year 4	Year 5
Accounts Profits	£1,758	£1,982	£1,561	£1,544	£1,892

TIMING DIFFERENCES

2.66 In arriving at these rule of 78 accounts profits (paragraph 2.50) there have been, on a cumulative basis to the ends of the years concerned, timing differences between the calculation of taxable profits (or losses) and the calculation of accounting profits. "Timing differences" are not an entirely straightforward concept, and we are often asked whether it is not possible to explain the calculation of deferred tax in some other way. It is not, because there is no other basis for the calculations which does not lead one into error in some circumstances. The only safe way of looking at the position is to compare at each accounting date the cumulative accounting charge, e.g. for depreciation, with the cumulative equivalent in tax terms, i.e. capital allowances.

a) Timing of difference on writing off capital expenditure

	Year 1	Year 2	Year 3	Year 4	Year 5
Tax allowance cumulatively	£100,000	£100,000	£100,000	£100,000	£100,000
Depreciation cumulatively	13,600	30,400	50,400	73,600	£100,000
	£86,400	£69,600	£49,600	£26,400	

b) Timing difference on relief for doubtful debts

Tax relief cumulatively	–	–	–	–	–
Accounts charge cumulatively	864	696	496	264	–
	£ 864	£ 696	£ 496	£ 264	–

c)

Total Timing difference	£ 85,536	£ 68,904	£ 49,104	£ 26,136	–

But to the extent of the tax losses carried forward from one year to the next, the lessor has not had any benefit from this accelerated availability of tax reliefs, compared with the slower expensing of the corresponding amounts in his profit and loss account.

2.67 It is only on the benefits he has had that a deferred tax charge is called for—that is on the excess of beneficial timing differences over unabsorbable losses, as follows:-

	Year 1	Year 2	Year 3	Year 4	Year 5
Timing difference (cumulative)	£85,536	£68,904	£49,104	£26,136	–
Losses to c/fwd per paragraph 2.62	£83,778	£65,164	£43,803	£19,291	–
Deferred tax to be provided on	£ 1,758	£ 3,740	£ 5.301	£ 6.845	–
Increase from year to year	£ 1,758	£ 1,982	£ 1,561	£ 1,544	

And if this last line has a familiar ring to it, it is because it is just that same line of accounts profits from the rule of 78 method with which we have been working throughout this exercise. It cannot be other.

THE DEFERRED TAX ACCOUNT

2.68 The deferred tax account, and the account for tax liability, are as follows:

			Deferred	Current
Year 1	£1,758 at 52%		£ 914	
Year 2	£1,982 at 52%		1,031	
		Balance being £3,740 at 52%	1,945	
Year 3	£1,561 at 52%		812	
		Balance being £5,301 at 52%	2,757	
Year 4	£1,544 at 52%		803	
		Balance being £6,845 at 52%	3,560	
Year 5	Tax to be provided on profits actually liable to tax £8,737 at 52%			£4,543
	Less release from deferred tax account		3,560	3,560
	Difference—net charge to profit and loss, being accounts profits £1,892 at 52%			983

2.69 In the preceding three paragraphs we have been looking at the deferred tax situation. It is now time, however, to examine tax based leasing with its rather different tax implications. As has already been indicated in Chapter I, the one single stimulus which has resulted in the very significant recent growth in the leasing industry has been the acceleration of tax allowances for expenditure on leased assets and the consequent possibility that the lessor may be able to take advantage more quickly (through his ability to absorb them elsewhere in his group) than the lessee.

TAX BASED LEASING—THE REVISED CASH FLOW FORECAST

2.70 If the lessor has taxable profits of a sufficient level at the commencement of the lease, he will be able to absorb, (and therefore will not need to carry forward,) his excess capital allowances in that year. The same principles apply to a lessor company which is a member of a group, and able to "surrender its losses" to a profit making company in that same group. We shall look in considerable detail in Chapter 5 at the technical tax position, but here we are dealing with the accounting situation. This is most easy to illustrate if we continue to look at the same individual lease as before, but assume that excess capital allowances are surrendered for "a payment for group relief" equal to their value in tax terms. It follows that the lease will thereafter generate tax profits which will not be capable of being offset by losses forward, since those losses are no longer available.

2.71 The revised cash flow forecast is as follows:-

	Rent (receivable) immediately before beginning of quarter	Tax payable (receivable) at beginning of quarter	Outstanding borrowing at beginning of quarter		Interest payable (receivable) at end of quarter	Outstanding borrowing at end of quarter
Year 1 Q1	(7,100)		92,900		3,251	96,151
Q2	(7,100)		89,051		3,117	92,168
Q3	(7,100)		85,068		2,977	88,045
Q4	(7,100)		80,945		2,833	83,778
					£12,178	
Year 2 Q1	(7,100)		76,678		2,684	79,362
Q2	(7,100)		72,262		2,529	74,791
Q3	(7,100)		67,691		2,369	70,060
Q4	(7,100)	(43,565)	19,395		679	20,074
					£ 8,261	
Year 3 Q1	(7,100)		12,974		454	13,428
Q2	(7,100)		6,328		222	6,550
Q3	(7,100)		(550)		(14)	(564)
Q4	(7,100)	10,472	2,808		98	2,906
				Pay	774	
				(Receive)	£(14)	
Year 4 Q1	(7,100)		(4,194)		£(105)	(4,299)
Q2	(7,100)		(11,399)		(285)	(11,684)
Q3	(7,100)		(18,784)		(470)	(19,254)
Q4	(7,100)	14,373	(11,981)		(300)	(12,281)
					£(1,160)	
Year 5 Q1	(7,100)		(19,381)		(485)	(19,866)
Q2	(7,100)		(26,966)		(674)	(27,640)
Q3	(7,100)		(34,740)		(869)	(35,609)
Q4	(7,100)	15,371	(27,338)		(683)	(28,021)
					£(2,711)	
Year 6 Q4		16,178				(11,843)

TAX CALCULATIONS

2.72 The tax calculations are as follows. The figures are worked out on the same straightforward basis which has already been illustrated in paragraph 2.62 above, although the results are obviously different not only because of the absence of losses available for carry forward, but also because of the different pattern of interest payments and receipts.

	Year 1	Year 2	Year 3	Year 4	Year 5
Rent	£28,400	£28,400	£28,400	£28,400	£28,400
Interest Paid	(12,178)	(8,261)	(774)		
Interest received			14	1,160	2,711
Capital allowances	(100,000)				
Profit		£20,139	£27,640	£29,560	£31,111
(Loss)	£(83,778)				
Liability		£10,472	£14,373	£15,371	£16,178
Group Relief Receipt	£(43,565)				

It is perhaps just worth reiterating that these tax figures remain unchanged whatever accounting method is used for the recognition of profit.

2.73 We can now put together the figures for profit and loss accounts of the tax based lease.

It is convenient to deal together with the annuity method figures, and those for the rule of 78. In each case the depreciation line remains unchanged from that previously shown in paragraphs 2.44 and 2.50 respectively. Readers will recall that the former was derived from a £92,900, 19 instalment annuity calculation, whilst the latter came from apportioning gross income into 20 quarterly parts. These bases remain valid: the lease is now tax based, but this does not change any of the factors upon which the calculations were originally made.

ACCOUNTS USING THE ANNUITY METHOD

2.74 The profit and loss account, using the annuity method, for a tax based lease appears as follows:-

	Year 1	Year 2	Year 3	Year 4	Year 5	Total
Rent	£28,400	£28,400	£28,400	£28,400	£28,400	£142,000
Depreciation	(14,204)	(16,645)	(19,506)	(22,858)	(26,787)	(100,000)
	£14,196	£11,755	£ 8,894	£ 5,542	£ 1,613	£ 42,000
Interest paid	(12,178)	(8,261)	(774)			(21,213)
Interest received	–	–	14	1,160	2,711	3,885
	£ 2,018	£ 3,494	£ 8,134	£ 6,702	£ 4,324	£ 24,672
Doubtful Debts	(858)	166	195	229	268	–
	£ 1,160	£ 3,660	£ 8,329	£ 6,931	£ 4,592	£ 24,672
Tax	(603)	(1,903)	(4,331)	(3,604)	(2,388)	(12,829)
	£ 557	£ 1,757	£ 3,998	£ 3,327	£ 2,204	£ 11,843

ACCOUNTS USING THE RULE OF 78 METHOD

2.75 Profit and loss account, using the rule of 78 method, for a tax based lease. (The income release calculations remain as illustrated in paragraph 2.50).

	Year 1	Year 2	Year 3	Year 4	Year 5	Total
Rent	£28,400	£28,400	£28,400	£28,400	£28,400	£142,000
Depreciation	(13,600)	(16,800)	(20,000)	(23,200)	(26,400)	(100,000)
	14,800	11,600	8,400	5,200	2,000	42,000
Interest Paid	(12,178)	(8,261)	(774)			(21,213)
Interest received			14	1,160	2,711	3,885
	2,622	3,339	7,640	6,360	4,711	24,672
Doubtful debts	(864)	168	200	232	264	–
	1,758	3,507	7,840	6,592	4,975	24,672
Tax	(914)	(1,823)	(4,077)	(3,428)	(2,587)	(12,829)
	£ 844	£ 1,684	£ 3,763	£ 3,164	£ 2,388	£ 11,843

2.76 The bottom lines of the annuity method profit and loss account, and that of the rule of 78, are not all that dissimilar.

In each case, the gross income line, (rent less depreciation), is slanted towards early release of income—the inclination of each line being exactly the same as it was in our earlier examination of these methods.

What has changed, now that we are looking at a tax based lease, is the pattern of interest payments. These decrease very fast after the first year, giving rise to heavy cash surpluses at a relatively early point in the lease term.

The result of this factor, in terms of the profit pattern as well as in the cash flow, is a "skewing" of the bottom line—it is the middle-to-end years rather than the early years in which the heavy amounts now fall.

The annuity method and the rule of 78 both suffer from this same defect. Although in a non-tax based lease each will produce an acceptable pattern of profits, their application in tax based leasing is rather less easy to justify.

When we turn to the investment period method, in paragraph 2.78, we will see an immediate difference. Use of that method causes profits to emerge on the bottom line which clearly bear some resemblance to the investment in the lease. This holds good for both tax based and non-tax based leases.

2.77 Before moving on to investment period, tax based, leases it is worth pausing for a minute to synthesise the tax figures used in these last two profit and loss accounts. Those worked out below are those under the rule of 78, but the principles are identical for the annuity method:-

	Deferred		Current	Net
Year 1				
Recovery (group relief) for which credit taken			£(43,565)	
Timing difference on asset	£86,400			
Timing difference on bad debt	(864)			£ 914
@ 52%	£85,536	£44,479		
Year 2				
Tax liability to be provided			10,472	
Reduction in timing diff. on asset	(16,800)			
Reduction in timing diff. on bad debt	168			1,823
@ 52%	£(16,632)	(8,649)		
Year 3				
Tax liability to be provided			14,373	
Reduction in timing diff. on asset	(20,000)			
Reduction in timing diff. on bad debt	200			4,077
	£(19,800)	(10,296)		
Year 4				
Tax liability to be provided			15,371	
Reduction in timing diff. on asset	(23,200)			
Reduction in timing diff. on bad debt	232			3,428
	£(22,968)	(11,943)		
Year 5				
Tax liability to be provided			16,178	
Reduction in timing diff. on asset	(26,400)			
Reduction in timing diff. on bad debt	264			2,587
	£(26,136)	(13,591)		
			£12,829	£12,829

TAX BASED LEASE—INVESTMENT PERIOD CALCULATIONS

2.78 The very important difference between the applications to tax based, as opposed to non-tax based, leases of the Investment Period method is that the period itself is different. In paragraph 2.53 above, we defined the period as starting at commencement of the lease and ending when cash flow moved from negative to positive. The cash flow in our tax based lease crosses that dividing line much earlier. (In fact it crosses it more than once, but it is normal practice to take the date of the final movement to the positive side of the line, i.e. the end of Year 3).

2.79 The calculations of the gross earnings to be reported in each year are therefore as follows:-

		Indebtedness at quarterly rests	Fraction for apportionment	Gross Earnings
Year 1	Q1	96,151	42,000:627,313	6,438
	Q2	92,168		6.171
	Q3	88,045		5,895
	Q4	83,778		5,609
				£24,113
Year 2	Q1	79,362		5,313
	Q2	74,791		5,007
	Q3	70,060		4,691
	Q4	20,074		1,344
				£16,355
Year 3	Q1	13,428		899
	Q2	6,550		438
	Q3	—		—
	Q4	2,906		195
				£ 1,532
		£627,313		£42,000

ACCOUNTS USING THE INVESTMENT PERIOD METHOD

2.80 Using these figures, the tax based lease, accounted for on the investment period method looks like this.

	Year 1	Year 2	Year 3	Year 4	Year 5	Total
Rent	£28,400	£28,400	£28,400	£28,400	£28,400	£142,000
Depreciation	(4,287)	(12,045)	(26,868)	(28,400)	(28,400)	(100,000)
	24,113	16,355	1,532			42,000
Interest payable	(12,178)	(8,261)	(774)			(21,213)
Interest receivable			14	1,160	2,711	3,885
	11,935	8,094	772	1,160	2,711	24,672
Doubtful debts	(957)	121	268	284	284	–
	10,978	8,215	1,040	1,444	2,995	24,672
Tax	(5,708)	(4,272)	(540)	(751)	(1,558)	(12,829)
	£ 5,270	£ 3,943	£ 500	£ 693	£ 1,437	£ 11,843

2.81 The net tax charge is made up of "current" and "deferred" elements as follows:-

Deferred	Year 1	Year 2	Year 3	Year 4	Year 5	Total
on asset	£95,713	£ (12,045)	£(26,868)	£(28,400)	£(28,400)	
on bad debts	(957)	121	268	284	284	
	£94,756	£ (11,924)	£(26,600)	£(28,116)	£(28,116)	
at 52%	49,273	(6,200)	(13,833)	(14,620)	(14,620)	
Current	(43,565)	10,472	14,373	15,371	16,178	12,829
	£ 5,708	£ 4,272	£ 540	£ 751	£ 1,558	£12,829

THE PATTERN OF INCOME RELEASE

2.82 The pattern of release of income, either at the pre-tax or post-tax line, now reflects the risk element relating to the investment in the lease. Thus the profits are highest in the early years when the investment and risks are greatest. In the fourth and fifth years when the cash position moves into surplus, the pre-tax income consists only of interest receivable plus releases from the doubtful debt provision. Rent and depreciation in these years are equal, so that there is no gross income needing recognition.

2.83 Opponents of the investment period method criticise the "front-end loading" of the income, criticising in particular the accounting exposure to bad debts in the later periods. This aspect will be examined in detail in the next chapter.

THE OVERALL VIEW

2.84 We have examined five methods of accounting. Of these, four, namely straight-line, annuity, reverse rule of 78 and investment period are in common use in the UK. The market value method is not often encountered, and we will not therefore pursue it further.

2.85 Let us consider what would be the effect on the published accounts of a lessor company of accounting under the different methods. We have illustrated one lease using each method, but what is the effect when numerous leases are being accounted for? Let us look first at the situation where the volume of business remains static and the flow of that business is regular.

NEW BUSINESS WITHOUT GROWTH

2.86 Under the straight-line method, using the pre-tax profit and loss figures from paragraph 2.09, and on the assumption that one new lease is written each year, the pattern of income can be tabulated as follows:-

	Year 1	Year 2	Year 3	Year 4	Year 5
First lease	£(4,578)	£(1,186)	£ 1,561	£ 4,712	£ 8,228
Second lease		(4,578)	(1,186)	1,561	4,712
Third lease			(4,578)	(1,186)	1,561
Fourth lease				(4.578)	(1.186)
Fifth lease					(4,578)
	£(4,578)	£(5,764)	£ (4,203)	£ 509	£ 8,737

Losses in the early years are heavy as new business is written. A small profit is recorded in Year 4, and a plateau reached in Year 5. Based on our assumptions, the income recognised would be constant thereafter.

2.87 Using the same method the income release can be quantified under each of the other methods, and we tabulate below the results of them all for comparison:

	Year 1	Year 2	Year 3	Year 4	Year 5
Straight-line	£(4,578)	£(5,764)	£(4,203)	£ 509	£8,737
Annuity	1,160	3,295	5,345	7,228	8,737
Rule of 78	1,758	3,740	5,301	6,845	8,737
Investment period	2,215	4,855	6,835	8,056	8,737

These are the non-tax based figures derived in paragraphs 2.44, 2.50 and 2.57 for the annuity, rule of 78 and investment period methods respectively. For completeness the tax based figures can also be set out, these being taken from paragraphs 2.74, 2.75 and 2.80 for the annuity, rule of 78, and the investment period methods:-

	Year 1	Year 2	Year 3	Year 4	Year 5
Annuity	£ 1,160	£ 4,820	£13,149	£20,080	£24,672
Rule of 78	1,758	5,265	13,105	19,697	24,672
Investment period	10,978	19,193	20,233	21,677	24,672

GROWTH IN NEW BUSINESS

2.88 The discrepancy between the different methods is considerable. It becomes even more marked if the assumptions are changed to illustrate a steady growth in business written. Assume that one new lease is written the first year, two in the second, three in the third and so on. The figures for pre-tax profit or loss appear as follows:-

	Year 1	Year 2	Year 3	Year 4	Year 5	Year 6
Non-tax based						
Straight-line	£(4,578)	£(10,342)	£(14,545)	£(14,036)	£(5,299)	£ 3,438
Annuity	1,160	4,455	9,800	17,028	25,765	34,502
Rule of 78	1,758	5,498	10,799	17,644	26,381	35,118
Investment period	2,215	7,070	13,905	21,961	30,698	39,435
Tax-based						
Annuity	1,160	5,980	19,129	39,209	63,881	88,553
Rule of 78	1,758	7,023	20,128	39,825	64,497	89,169
Investment period	10,978	30,171	50,404	72,081	96,753	121,425

2.89 The disparity is quite startling. In the non-tax based versions, the straight-line method produces losses in each of the first five years, some of them quite large. It seems nonsensical that writing profitable leases (which these are) can be accounted for truly and fairly showing losses of these magnitudes. The annuity method,the rule of 78 and the investment period method produce, as one would expect in non-tax based leasing, results which are fairly similar. The profits show a steady increase reflecting the increase in business. In the tax-based figures, profits under the annuity method and the rule of 78 are low in the early years, but the investment period method shows a steady pattern of increase throughout.

THE INVESTMENT PERIOD RESULTS AND THOSE OF EXCESSIVE PRUDENCE

2.90 Thus, in an expanding business that is writing non-tax based leasing, the annuity method, the rule of 78 or the investment period method seem to give a fair indication of the underlying profit trend. For tax-based leasing we firmly believe that the investment period method produces the most appropriate answer. An expansionist lessor, confident in his ability to maintain his growth rate, and unafraid of showing maximum earnings would probably choose the investment period method, whilst an excessively prudent organisation wanting to defer recognition of its profits until the latest possible point would use the straight-line method.

DECLINE AND FALL

2.91 But what happens when a business declines or ceases? Let us suppose in each of the cases illustrated in paragraph 2.88 above that no new business is written after the sixth year.
The figures run off as follows:-

	Year 6 as before	Year 7	Year 8	Year 9	Year 10
Non-tax based					
Straight-line	£ 3,438	£ 44,221	£ 65,838	£69,412	£49,368
Annuity	34,502	35,119	27,751	18,843	9,054
Rule of 78	35,118	31,549	24,654	18,724	11,352
Investment period	39,435	32,667	20,709	10,731	4,086
Tax-based					
Annuity	88,553	105,105	102,997	64,546	27,552
Rule of 78	89,169	101,535	99,900	64,427	29,850
Investment period	121,425	69,251	25,440	23,639	17,970

2.92 Inevitably, the pattern of income recognition now reverses. The profits not previously released under the straight-line method come through, masking the actual decline in business. The masking effect is considerably less under the other three methods. However, it is noticeable that no losses appear under any method in any year whereas in the growth years illustrated in paragraph 2.88 losses resulted from using the straight-line method.

2.93 It is easy to forget in all these figures that the total income for the non-tax based leases under each method over the ten year period is £183,477—a profit of £8,737 on each of 21 leases. Similarly, the tax-based lease profits total £518,112, however these are accounted for.

COMPARISONS

2.94 Where does this leave us? Since all of the above methods are used by UK leasing companies, it is apparent that reasonable comparison of the accounts of different companies is not possible where they themselves recognise their income under different sets of rules. Indeed, it is not possible to make meaningful comparisons even of the accounts of two companies using the straight-line method unless those companies are themselves at the same stage in their business cycle.

THE AUTHORS' VIEWS

2.95 It seems to us that all these figures confirm our view that the straight-line method releases income in a manner unrelated to underlying facts. The annuity, the rule of 78 and the investment period method all produce acceptable results for non-tax based leases, but the last must be preferred for tax-based leasing.

THE METHODS COMMONLY USED IN PRACTICE

2.96 Which accounting methods do the individual UK leasing companies use? This is very difficult to say because the accounting policies disclosed in the accounts are often sufficiently ambiguous to be interpreted as a description of more than one of the methods. However we believe that only a small number of UK lessors are using the straight-line method. The annuity method seems to be in fairly common use, particularly for large, one-off contracts, (often referred to as "big ticket" deals). The most common method is undoubtedly the rule of 78, both for tax-based and non tax-based leases. But the investment period method is gradually gaining ground, as lessors come to acknowledge that it rests squarely upon the principles upon which they make the decision on the terms on which they can write leases. It is the basis of the published accounts of only a small number of companies, but is used by considerably more as a management reporting method. It is seen as particularly appropriate by the leasing subsidiaries of clearing banks, who have long regarded finance leasing as primarily another form of their bank's lending. We are also aware that proposed changes of accounting method under consideration by a number of lessors have been held back, awaiting the promised Statement of Standard Accounting Practice. An exposure draft has been in the offing for some considerable time, and is now expected to be published in late 1978.

THE BALANCE SHEET TREATMENT

2.97 We have referred in this chapter many times to the recording of the asset in the lessor's books, and to the methods of depreciating it. It is the general practice in the UK either to treat it as a fixed asset, or to classify it as a leased asset and to place it between fixed and current assets in the balance sheet. This treatment is often adopted because lessors fear that if the leased assets were not shown as fixed, or at least non-current assets, the Inland Revenue might refuse to accept that the assets are fixed assets of the lessor used in his trade, rather than used in that of the lessee. We will look at the technical tax position, and in particular at the fixed asset problem, in chapter 5.

In a few cases the leased assets are shown in the balance sheet as a debtor. The figure is the same but is represented as the aggregate of rental payments yet to be received less a provision for unearned income. Whilst this is the presentation which we prefer for finance leases we have in the examples in this book used the more usual UK practice of showing the assets as fixed assets.

2.98 The standard American practice, which we shall consider further in chapter 6, is the latter. They treat all assets subject to finance leases as debtors, the balance sheet figure being shown net of unearned income. This figure is then split between the amounts of rentals currently due and those that are non-current, depending upon the due date of the lease rentals. Those due within one year of balance sheet date are classified as current, whilst all others are non-current.

DISTINGUISHING FINANCE AND OPERATING LEASES

2.99 Throughout this chapter, we have assumed that the leases in question are finance (or full pay-out) leases. As we have already pointed out in paragraph 1.04 these are essentially for the whole of the life of the asset and they imply that the lessor effectively gives up most of the rights of ownership, and views the deal as a loan of money for interest.

2.100 However, the lessor may not always see things this way. Unlike the U.S., there are no rules in the UK laying down which leases are to be considered finance leases and which are to be considered operating leases. Accordingly each lessor has to decide for himself. Normally under an operating lease the lessor retains some of the owner's risks, such as that of obsolescence, and also bears the burden of repairs and insurance. By far the most usual distinguishing mark of an operating lease is the fact that the lease term is a period shorter than the full anticipated life of the asset. From the outset the lessor expects the asset to revert to him after the term expires, and then expects to be able to re-lease to a new lessee for some part of the remainder of the asset's life. The lease cannot thus be looked upon as a financing transaction, but is a means of employing assets to earn profit.

2.101 The distinction between the two types of lease is often not clear cut. A lessor may grant a lease for a period of five years, using in his calculations a residual value for the asset of 50% of cost. He may have no intention of re-leasing the asset at the end of this period, but take the view that inflation will have increased the residual value enabling him to sell in such a way as to produce a (historic cost accounting) "profit". Is such a lease a finance lease? Probably, but the lessor concerned can always argue that he views it as an operating lease. Under American rules it would probably not be a finance lease.

ACCOUNTING FOR OPERATING LEASES

2.102 We must now consider what is the appropriate accounting treatment for operating leases in the books of a lessor.

2.103 The principle of accounting for operating leases is that the lessor capitalises the asset at cost as a fixed asset and depreciates it in the same way as he would any other fixed asset of similar type. Rentals are credited to income, normally on an accruals basis, as they fall due. All costs including initial costs, are charged against income when incurred. No provision is created against doubtful debts, except in respect of rentals due but unpaid.

2.104 Let us assume the same basic figures as we used in paragraph 2.07 for our finance lease, but in this case take it that the initial lease is for a period of only three years. The asset is then re-leased on similar terms to a different lessee for the remaining two years. The lessor's policy is to depreciate all fixed assets straight-line over their effective life.

THE LESSOR'S PROFIT AND LOSS ACCOUNT AND BALANCE SHEET

2.105 The profit and loss account and balance sheet will look like this:-

Profit and Loss	Year 1	Year 2	Year 3	Year 4	Year 5	Total
Rent	£28,400	£28,400	£28,400	£28,400	£28,400	£142,000
Depreciation	(20,000)	(20,000)	(20,000)	(20,000)	(20,000)	(100,000)
	8,400	8,400	8,400	8,400	8,400	42,000
Interest payable	(12,178)	(9,786)	(7,039)	(3,888)	(372)	(33,263)
	£(3,778)	£(1,386)	£ 1,361	£ 4,512	£ 8,028	£ 8,737
Balance sheet at year end						
Fixed asset—at cost less depreciation	£80,000	£60,000	£40,000	£20,000	–	

2.106 This of course closely resembles the finance lease accounted for under the straight-line method, with the omission of the provision for doubtful debts. In practice, the rentals for an operating lease are likely to be higher than those for a finance lease for two reasons:-

1. The lessor risks being unable to re-lease the asset at the end of the initial period, or sell at the value implicit in the lease, either through lack of demand for the type of asset, or because it has become obsolete;

2. The lessor will often be responsible for repairs and maintenance, and will therefore need to cover his anticipated expenditure on them in setting the lease rental.

THE NECESSITY FOR DISTINGUISHING OPERATING FROM FINANCE LEASES

2.107 In the U.S., the distinction between a finance lease and an operating lease has become important for two reasons:-

1. A totally different method of income recognition is prescribed for the two types

2. The balance sheet treatment is also different.

2.108 As we have just seen, the methods of income recognition and balance sheet presentation in the UK can be very similar. Differentiating the two types of lease has not therefore been of paramount importance. As regards income recognition, with the increasing trend towards the annuity, the rule of 78 and investment period methods for finance leases, there will increasingly be a need to segregate the two types. But this distinction will only be final and complete when each is afforded different treatment in the balance sheet.

2.109 Since there are no rules relating to the treatment of leases in the UK, lessors and lessees have been able to exploit the situation each to his own advantage. It is quite possible at present for a lessor to treat a lease as a financing transaction and at the same time for the lessee to keep the transaction off balance sheet. Equally, it is possible though less likely, for a lessee to capitalise a lease which the lessor regards as an operating lease. We shall be looking further at this question as it relates to lessees in chapter 4, but first we must consider some specific problems which affect the lessor and his accounting methods.

CHAPTER 3 – SPECIFIC ACCOUNTING PROBLEMS

Contents

LEASES BY MANUFACTURERS

3.01 An increasing amount of leasing business in the UK is being written by manufacturers as a means of selling their own products. Sometimes the leases are written in the name of the manufacturing company, sometimes in the name of a separate company set up for the purpose. How should the manufacturer-lessor divide his aggregate profit between the sale of his product on the one hand, and the financing of that sale on the other, and when should he recognise each element?

FINANCE LEASES

3.02 Accountants are usually taught that it is incorrect to "capitalise profit" on work done for oneself. Text books show examples of companies building their own machines, and tell the reader to reduce the figure of "cost" to that of cost to the company. If this analogy were followed through into the area now being considered, it would indicate that the manufacturer should transfer the item at cost to his leasing associate, recognising no profit himself. He would leave the whole profit to filter into the leasing associate's profit and loss account over a period of years under one of the accepted lease accounting methods.

3.03 But the manufacturer-lessor who concludes a finance lease with his customer can properly claim that he has disposed of his interest in the goods. He retains some rights against the lessee should the latter fail to pay the lease rentals, but these rights are not significantly different from those resulting from an outright sale. It therefore seems appropriate to segregate the two transactions—one being the sale by the manufacturer of his usual product, and the other a financing transaction relating to the sale. Thus the normal manufacturing profit would be recognised at the time the lease was entered into, and the finance profit over the term of the lease.

3.04 There are certain conditions which must be fulfilled before a lessor should recognise his manufacturing profit. The first is that recoverability of the lease rentals should not be in any greater doubt than usual. The second is that there are no major costs connected with the asset which the manufacturer-lessor still has to incur. If there are any such costs, profit recognition should be delayed until such time as they have been incurred or can be reliably estimated. Thirdly, and most importantly, the finance lease part of the transaction must stand on its own, that is to say it must be calculated on an underlying rate which is comparable to rates quoted by independent lessors for similar finance.

CALCULATING THE FIGURES

3.05 In practice, a manufacturer-lessor who has arranged a finance lease of a product would first segregate the arrangement into two parts. He would establish what is his normal manufacturing profit on the product, which should be relatively easy. Let us assume that his cost of manufacture is £80,000, and that he would normally sell at a figure 40% up on that, i.e. £112,000. If this is the figure he has used as his "cost" for fixing the finance lease rentals he has merely to establish that the rate of interest implicit in the lease is comparable to that being offered by other lessors.

REDUCING PROFIT FOR LEASES WHICH SUBSIDISE THE SALE

3.06 If he can substantiate his implicit rate, he will then be able to recognise his manufacturing profit immediately and the lease can be regarded as a separate transaction. Where the comparable rate is lower than his own, he may congratulate himself on having concluded a satisfactory deal, recognise his full manufacturer's profit, and look forward to bonus profits over the lease period.

3.07 If, on the other hand, he finds that the comparable rate is higher than his own, he must make further calculations to enable him to calculate his true manufacturers profit. He will calculate first the present value of the lease rentals using that higher comparable interest rate. The present value which results is then compared with his manufacturing costs. The difference between these two represents the manufacturing profit actually achieved. Since it will in these circumstances inevitably be lower than his normal manufacturing profit level, he should recognise only the lower amount.

3.08 Illustrating this in the figures already quoted, let us assume that the lease is a full pay out lease for five years at a quarterly rental in advance of £7,100. This represents a yield of 2.645% per quarter, equivalent almost exactly to 11% per annum on the "cost" of £112,000. Investigation reveals that the comparable cost of similar funds from other lessors would be 13%. He therefore discounts the rentals at this rate to arrive at a present value of approximately £100,000. The effect is that he has reduced his "deemed" selling price from £112,000 to £100,000. His manufacturing profit available to be recognised is £20,000 instead of £32,000. The remainder of the profit will be recognised over the period of the lease, by one of the methods outlined in chapter 2.

OPERATING LEASES

3.09 The whole of the foregoing contrasts with the position where the manufacturer-lessor supplies his product to a customer by way of an operating lease. Here the manufacturer cannot be said to have disposed of his interest in the goods. He has appropriated them to a different category of asset, namely a fixed asset rather than inventory, and he still retains many of the risks of ownership. It can be strongly argued that in these circumstances the lessor has not done anything which entitles him to recognise a manufacturing profit. When the lease is short these arguments have even more force. An analogy can be drawn with our earlier example of the company which built its own machines (see paragraph 3.02). In both cases, the assets are being used, hopefully, to earn profits for the business.

3.10 The counter argument can best be demonstrated by first looking at a case in which it is universally agreed that it would not be correct to recognise a manufacturing profit, and then looking at a case where it would be correct. First there is the case of Company A, which builds a machine which is to be used in its own business. Company A's hope is, of course, that this business will produce larger profits as a result, but it would not recognise any part of these profits when it had completed building the machine. Contrast this with Company B, which builds a machine to be leased out on a series of operating leases. It is argued that these two companies' positions are not analogous. The machine-building activity of Company B is a part of its trade which should be looked at as if it were a separate, independent, activity. Similarly the leasing activity should be looked at independently. It is therefore said to be wrong to pretend that the machine-building is an activity not designed to produce profit. It is also argued that failing to recognise a machine-building profit has the effect of understating the real loss which results if the machine is not leased out for any part of its subsequent life.

The decision whether profits should be recognised by a manufacturer-lessor on his manufacturing activity, when he intends that his leasing will be by way of operating leases, is a finely balanced one. We take the view that he should not recognise any manufacturing profit.

GOVERNMENT GRANTS

3.11 The lessor who is entitled to a Government grant for the asset he purchases is in no different a position from any other grant recipient. Grants are normally between 20% and 30% of the capital cost. Although they are tax free, capital allowances are nevertheless available in many cases on the full asset cost.

In practical terms, the most important effect for the recipient is his considerably reduced need for borrowed funds. A lessor must reflect his lowered costs in the terms he offers to a potential lessee, if that lessee is to see them as comparable to his own outgoings were he to purchase outright.

ACCOUNTING FOR GOVERNMENT GRANTS (S.S.A.P. No.4)

3.12 The lessor who receives a grant can account for it in either of the alternative ways permitted under Statement of Standard Accounting Practice No. 4, The Accounting Treatment of Government Grants, (S.S.A.P. 4).

One method is to reduce the asset cost shown in the balance sheet by the amount of the grant. The profit and loss result of this is that depreciation is required only to write off that reduced cost over the asset's life.

3.13 The alternative, which is the method generally adopted by lessors, is to leave the asset's cost unreduced in the balance sheet, and to credit the grant to a "deferred income account" placed on the balance sheet between shareholders' funds and other liabilities.

Releases are made annually from deferred income into profit and loss account. Depreciation is charged by reference to the full cost of the asset. Therefore, mathematically, the net impact on profit and loss account of the two methods will be the same.

3.14 The choice of this second method by the majority of lessors is based on two factors. First, from the viewpoint of showing all leased assets in a consistent manner in the balance sheet, it seems more reasonable not to take the grant off the asset cost. This argument has less force in the case of recipients other than lessors, since the numbers of assets involved, and the even smaller numbers of grants received, pose fewer presentational problems.

Secondly, lessors would generally feel it more appropriate to recognise that a grant was an element of income, and not a reduction of costs. Once again other recipients might be less compelled by this thinking.

DISTORTIONS IN THE TAX CHARGE

3.15 The accounting distortion which does need consideration arises from the tax free characteristic of the grants. Whether the grant filters into profit and loss account by means of a reduced depreciation charge, or as a release of deferred income, it comes into the pre-tax part of the account. Since it is not subject to tax, the tax charge appears to be lower than 52% of pre-tax income.

3.16 This can be illustrated more clearly using the deferred income release method, and taking two hypothetical year's figures:

	Year 1	Year 2
Profit (Loss) before grant credit	£100	£(300)
Government Grant credit	200	200
Pre-tax profit (Loss)	300	(100)
Tax (payable) recoverable	(52)	156
Post-tax profit	£248	£ 56

ENGROSSMENT OF THE GRANT CREDIT

3.17 A solution which is being adopted by an increasing number of lessors is to present the grant credit in the profit and loss account at an engrossed amount. The figures would appear thus:-

	Year 1	Year 2
Profit (Loss) before grant credit	£100	£(300)
Government Grant credit	417	417
Pre-tax profit	517	117
Tax at 52%	(269)	(61)
Post-tax profit	£248	£ 56

£417 is the grant of £200 engrossed at 52% and the tax charge includes £217 of notional tax on that engrossed amount. The balance of the tax charge is of course the real tax liability and recovery shown in the previous paragraph.

3.18 Some lessors, and their auditors, consider that engrossment is contrary to S.S.A.P. 4. That standard refers to "a deferred credit, a portion of which is released to revenue annually". The word "revenue" is taken to mean pre-tax profit, but the standard does not in fact consider the tax free nature of the grants.

We believe that grossing up grants is not prevented by S.S.A.P. 4. But, as the matter is not free from doubt, it would be helpful if the Accounting Standards Committee were to clarify this point.

BAD AND DOUBTFUL DEBTS

3.19 In the examples in Chapter 2, we illustrated the provision for doubtful debts at a rate of 1 percent. Experience indicates that a provision of between 1% and 2% of the figure at which the asset is stated in the balance sheet is adequate to deal with the bad debts to be anticipated on a normal leasing book. But on a tax based lease accounted for by the investment period method, there is no gross income, that is rental income less depreciation, after the investment period has ended. The only income then flowing into profit and loss account is the interest received on the surplus cash "invested". Should a bad debt occur in this period, it will show up as an impact on profit and loss account, not reduced by gross income, and only to a relatively small extent covered by the doubtful debts provision then remaining.

ACCOUNTING EXPOSURE

3.20 Critics of the investment period method point to this bad debt exposure in the latter part of a lease as an argument that the lessor should not be permitted to "front end" the lease income in the way which results from using the investment period method. Prudence, they say, requires the income to be spread over all periods whilst there is risk. It is undeniable that risk is still present after all the income has been recognised. It is, however, true that under any of the recognised accounting methods the incidence of a bad debt in the later stages of a lease would in all probability create a loss substantially in excess of future income. The problem is thus one of degree, not of absolutes. It needs also to be borne in mind that the amounts of interest income generated in the later stages of a lease after the investment period has ended may be quite substantial and that these would mitigate a loss to some extent.

ADEQUACY OF THE GENERAL PROVISION, AND THE NEED FOR SPECIFIC PROVISIONS

3.21 In our view the question of bad debts is one which is entirely separate from that of how to account for lease income. In a trading situation, the fact that a debt may become uncollectible does not prevent the recording of a sale—it merely affects the level of doubtful debt provision at the time that recoverability comes into question. Similarly, under a lease, the provision for irrecoverability should be made at the time the future rentals are detected as doubtful. Here, prudence demands that the level of general provision for doubtful debts should always be closely scrutinised for adequacy. But that this is even more necessary when using the investment period method.

EVALUATING THE RISK AND THE SECURITY HELD

3.22 In assessing the bad debt risk, the value of the underlying asset for potential re-leasing needs to be considered if repossession is legally and technically possible. An asset which is only capable of being used by one lessee, or by a small group of people, is a greater risk than would be a motor car. With very large single lease items, such as aircraft and ships, it is unlikely that any lessor could build up from his total leasing book an adequate general provision to sustain a default on one such item. A loss would normally have to be taken in the profit and loss account as and when it arose. Many lessors have kept clear of the larger risks for this reason, knowing that a loss of that size could place their whole business in jeopardy. This is a main cause of the formation of consortia for leasing large assets, so as to spread the risks in smaller amounts across more assets and between more lessors.

3.23 The quantification of the necessary provision for doubtful debts will also require an assessment of the realisable value of the leased asset, whether on sale or re-leasing. This is particularly difficult for assets whose value moves in sympathy with market conditions, for instance ships. Consequent fluctuations in doubtful debt provisions can severely distort the profit and loss account. There may thus be a case to be made out for failing to reduce a provision once made, even if an asset has regained its value. The provision would stand until the asset's eventual realisation. Whatever view is taken its application must be consistent.

CURRENCY LEASES

3.24 In what follows we will use the phrase "currency leases" to describe those leases where all the main constituent elements, (borrowing for the purchase of the asset, interest thereon, and rental receipts), are not sterling, but are in the same foreign currency. We will assume that the lessor accounts in sterling. The accounting problems arising in such currency leases relate mainly to the *translation* of currency figures into sterling for the purpose of preparing accounts. The quite separate process of *converting* currencies (on remittance) is usually a very much smaller area of difficulty.

In paragraph 3.42 below, and the succeeding paragraphs, we will deal with multi-currency leases, namely those in which part or all of borrowing, interest and/or rentals is in a second currency. The second currency may or may not be sterling (in which we will again assume the lessor to account).

REAL EXPOSURE, ACCOUNTING EXPOSURE AND TAX DIFFICULTIES

3.25 The real exposure to currency movements and what we may call the accounting exposure are frequently entirely different. Exposure to tax charges, or to unavailability of tax reliefs may well be different again; our tax legislation in this area has not evolved with the speed and flexibility necessary to cope with the complexities of modern business.

The only safe course is analysis. Work out your actual exposure at each point in the time-span of your proposed transaction. Analyse it in terms of the effect on profit and loss account and balance sheet. What will happen if the transaction needs to be closed off at some point when rates are not what were expected? Also work out how the accounts will reflect the uncompleted transaction at each year end under normal methods of translation of currency to sterling. Lastly, look carefully at the impact of taxation on the transaction if completed, or if closed prematurely, and also on those intermediate profits and losses thrown up by translation.

Tax implications will largely be left to chapter 5 and are only briefly referred to in this chapter. What we will mainly be examining in depth are the accounting aspects.

THE REASONS FOR CURRENCY LEASES

3.26 There are numerous reasons why it may seem advantageous to borrow currency to finance leasing transactions, but the two most commonly met in practice are as follows:-

a) The lessee wishes to pay the rental in a foreign currency
b) Favourable borrowing rates

3.27 A lessee whose operations generate a flow of foreign currency income may wish to limit his exposure in that currency by using that currency or some part of it to obtain the use of the assets with which it is generated. The lessor who wants to do business with this lessee may well, in his turn, borrow currency to finance his asset purchase, thinking that the future rentals will fairly cover the loan repayments and interest needing to be paid in the future. His exposure is not quite so straightforward, as we shall see.

3.28 The other main reason for a lessor borrowing foreign currency is because favourable borrowing rates may be available in that currency. This occurs particularly in relation to ships. Many governments subsidise their national shipbuilding industries by making available loans at favourable rates of interest to purchasers of the ships concerned. In this case it may well be the lessor who seeks a lessee willing to pay the rentals in a foreign currency matching that of the original loan thereby reducing his, the lessor's currency exposure risk.

THE BASIC EXAMPLE AGAIN

3.29 Let us assume that the full cost of the leased asset has been borrowed in dollars, and that the rents are also denominated in dollars.

At an exchange rate of $2 = £1, the first year's cash flow is easy to derive from the data previously illustrated in paragraph 2.08—these being the figures of our basic example, in which tax was ignored.

		Rent receivable immediately before beginning of quarter	Outstanding borrowing at beginning of quarter	Interest payable at end of quarter	Outstanding borrowing at end of quarter
Year 1					
	Q1	$14,200	$185,800	$6,502	$192,302
	Q2	14,200	178,102	6,234	184,336
	Q3	14,200	170,136	5,954	176,090
	Q4	14,200	161,890	5,666	167,556

Over the period of the lease a profit of $17,474 will emerge. We assume that dollars of rent received are each promptly used to pay interest and repay borrowings. Therefore the profit will emerge in terms of cash flow in year 5, the amounts being $2,848 in the third quarter, and $14,626 in the fourth.

3.30 On the assumption that rents are used to pay off borrowings and interest the profit cannot be other than $17,474. The sterling accounts would recognise this, at the translation rates used for each year's accounts. The years in which it filtered into the pre-tax line in the profit and loss account would be the same as before.

EXCHANGE RATE CHANGES—THE ASSET TREATED AS A CURRENCY ASSET

3.31 What would be the effect if the exchange rate moved, before the end of year 1, to \$1.80 = £1? Using the figures calculated in paragraph 2.57 (the investment period method using quarterly rests), the profit and loss account and balance sheet figures for year 1 would be as follows:-

Rent		\$56,800		£31,555
Depreciation		26,276		14,598
		30,524		16,957
Interest	24,356		13,531	
Doubtful debts	1,737	26,093	965	14,496
		\$ 4,431		£ 2,461
Asset cost		200,000		111,111
Less depreciation		26,276		14,598
		\$173,724		£96,513

3.32 The right hand column translates all of the dollar figures at an assumed rate of \$1.80 = £1. The liabilities and assets sides of the balance sheet balance with no exchange difference:-

Retained earnings	£2,461	**Asset (cost less depreciation)**	£96,513
Doubtful debt provision	965		
Borrowing (\$167,556 at 1.80)	93,087		
	£96,513		£96,513

The absence of any exchange difference should not surprise us.

3.33 If there should be any reader who wonders whether there should not have been a difference, the following should make it clear. The profit and loss account and balance sheet figures are in this case put together on the footing that there were already sterling figures in the books, at \$2 = £1, before the year end accounts were prepared:-

PROFIT AND LOSS	
Rents received \$56,800 @ \$1.80	£ 31,555
(originally £28,400—difference £3,155)	
Depreciation \$26,276 @ \$1.80	(14,598)
	16,957
Interest paid \$24,356 @ \$1.80	(13,531)
(originally £12,178—difference £1,353)	
	3,426
Doubtful debts \$1,737 @ \$1.80	(965)
RETAINED EARNINGS	£ 2,461
BALANCE SHEET	
Loan—\$167,556 @ \$1.80	
(originally £83,778—difference £9,309)	£ 93,087
Doubtful debts provision \$1,737 @ \$1.80	965
Retained earnings	2,461
TOTAL OF LIABILITIES SIDE	£ 96,513
Asset—cost \$200,000 @ \$1.80	£111,111
(originally £100,000—difference £11,111)	
Less depreciation \$26,276 @ \$1.80	14,598
Total of assets side	£ 96,513

The four exchange difference figures, (one sided credits of £11,111 and £1,353, and one sided debits of £3,155 and £9,309), cancel each other out.

TREATING THE ASSET AS A STERLING ASSET

3.34 There is however another possibility. If having acquired the asset for $200,000 the lessor decided to regard it as a sterling asset and not a dollar one, then his profit and loss account and balance sheet would be different again:-

PROFIT AND LOSS	
Rents received $56,800 @ $1.80	£ 31,555
Depreciation (sterling figure taken from paragraph 2.57)	(13,138)
	18,417
Interest paid $24,356 @ $1.80	(13,531)
	4,886
Doubtful debts provision (sterling)	(869)
Pre tax profit, (before dealing with exchange adjustment)	£ 4,017
BALANCE SHEET	
Loan—$167,556 @ $1.80	£ 93,087
Doubtful debt provision	869
Pre tax profit (before dealing with exchange adjustment	4,017
TOTAL LIABILITIES SIDE	£ 97,973
Asset—cost	£100,000
Less depreciation	(13,138)
	£ 86,862

It is immediately apparent that:-

a) the profit is greater by £1,556 than it was in our previous example;

b) an exchange adjustment of £11,111 (Deficit) needs to be dealt with.

The latter would be written off, either through reserves or profit and loss account, according to company policy.

The accounting treatment adopted above is more usual than that set out in paragraph 3.31. Asset costs are more often recorded in sterling terms, and depreciation calculated in sterling, despite the arguments that leases such as this should be regarded as wholly a currency transaction.

IS IT TRUE AND FAIR TO TREAT THE ASSET AS A STERLING ONE

3.35 We, however, believe that the method of accounting set out in the preceding paragraph, albeit one normally met, is wrong in circumstances in which it is clear that the lessor will not actually suffer a loss of £11,111. The case shown is one in which no such loss can occur. The apparent loss has arisen as a result of treating the asset as having had a sterling cost rather than a currency one.

If the asset is to be treated in this way, it is reasonable in our view for an exchange suspense account (debit) to be carried in the balance sheet.

3.36 The profit and loss account would now appear as follows:-

Rents received $56,8000 @ $1.80	£31.555
Depreciation (sterling figure taken from paragraph 2.57)	(13,138)
	18,417
Interest paid $24,356 @ $1.80	(13,531)
	4,886
Doubtful debts provision (sterling)	(869)
	4,017
Less exchange adjustment	1,556
	£ 2,461

It is clear from this that we see no valid reason why the profit figure should differ from that shown in paragraph 3.31.

The balance sheet would include the following:

Liabilities side		**Assets side**	
Profit and loss	£ 2,461	**Asset at cost less depreciation**	£86,862
Loan	93,087	**Exchange suspense account**	9,555
Doubtful debt provision	869		
	£96,417		£96,417

The aggregate of the release from exchange suspense account into profit and loss, £1,556, and the remaining balance on that account, £9,555, is the familiar figure of £11,111.

TAX PROBLEMS

3.37 The tax problem, whose solution we will leave to chapter 5, can be shortly stated. If the exchange rate remains constant at $1.80 = £1 for the remainder of the lease, the elements of the lessors tax computation will be:-

Five years rentals $284,000 @ $1.80		£157,775
Less Capital Allowances—original cost of asset $200,000 at then rate $2.00	£100,000	
Five years interest $66,526 @ $1.80	36,956	136,956
		£ 20,819
Tax on this, at 52% would be	10,826	
The total cash generated by the lease is however $17.474 @ $1.80	9,708	
Shortfall	£ 1,118	

What would be required to restore sanity to the above would be tax deductibility for the "loss" on repayment of the loan—£11,111 in sterling terms. The pre-tax profit would then be £9.708, which is the translation at $1.80 of the actual dollar profit of $17,474. The tax deduction for loan losses is in the Revenue's view dependent upon the nature of that borrowing ("Fixed Capital" or "Circulating")—common sense does not necessarily help. We look at this tax problem in its proper context in paragraphs 5.48 to 5.50.

CURRENCY ADJUSTMENT CLAUSES

3.38 The last seven paragraphs have looked at the attempt of a lessor to protect himself against risks by using the same currency for rents and borrowings.

There is an entirely different way in which he can organise his affairs, namely a clause in the lease, (or an agreement outside it,) that the lessee should reimburse the lessor with any additional sterling costs of interest and loan repayment paid in currency. Similarly, should the lessor make a profit on these items, he will account for it to the lessee.

Such a "currency adjustment clause" normally requires that the adjusting payments be made at the time the lessor would wish to make the interest payments and loan repayments envisaged in his original lease calculations. He is therefore able to keep both his profit and loss account and his cash flow unchanged.

3.39 We can illustrate the effect of all these currency adjustments as follows. The lessor has once again borrowed $200,000, and purchased an asset which he carries in his books at its original cost of £100,000. His rents are to be received in sterling.

His profit and loss account for the first year shows;-
shows:-

Rents (received in sterling)		£28,400
Depreciation (provided in sterling)		13,138
		15,262
Interest $24,356 @ $1.80	£13.531	
Less received from lessee	1,353	12,178
		3,084
Doubtful debt provision (in sterling)		869
		£ 2,215

3.40 The borrowing, and repayments thereof, are dealt with as follows in the books

Original borrowing @ $2.00	£100,000	$200,000
Repayments in year out of lessor's funds @ 1.80	16,222	29,200
out of lessee's funds @ 1.80 £1,802		3.244
	83,778	$167,556
Exchange difference—to revalue to $1.80 the outstanding borrowing	9,309	
	£ 93,087	

In his balance sheet, the lessor must show his liability to the overseas lender at £93,087. However, since he knows that he can look to the lessee for any excess over £83,778, he will quite properly show the difference, £9,309 as a receivable—an asset representing the right to call on the lessee for that sum.

3.41 Summarising these figures, the lessor's balance sheet at the end of year 1 will show:-

Profit and loss	£ 2,215	**asset cost less depreciation**	£86,862
doubtful debt provision	869	**receivable from lessee**	9,309
borrowing	93,087		
	£96,171		£96,171

The lessee has paid, and will charge in his profit and loss account as "rent" (albeit it includes the extra amounts called for under the currency adjustment clause),

normal rent	£28,400
additional amount for interest	1,353
additional amount for repayment	1,802
	£31,555

Perhaps it will once again come as no particular surprise that if the rents had been denominated in dollars, at $56,800 per annum, the lessee would have needed £31.555 in order to acquire at $1.80 those necessary dollars.

The tax position of both lessor and lessee as a result of these payments is a matter to which we will return in paragraphs 5.58 et seq. below.

MULTI-CURRENCY LEASES

3.42 We have so far only illustrated the position where leases are wholly financed in a single currency. It is the usual practice, however, for financing to be arranged partly in one currency and partly in another; or to be arranged in one currency with an option for the lender to call for repayment in another.

SYMMETRY AND ASYMMETRY

3.43 The exposure to which the lessor, (or lessee), leaves himself open in this case is not quite so simple a matter as those we have examined so far.

The additional complication may be called the lease's symmetry or asymmetry. The meaning of these words will be clear from the following assumptions, and so will their implications. Let us assume that one half of the borrowing is made in dollars, and that one half of the rents are received in dollars. At the time at which the original borrowing took place, the exchange rate was $2.00 = £1, and this rate continued to apply until the third quarter of year 3. Immediately after the end of that quarter, the rate moved to $1.80 = £1. This latter rate remained constant throughout the remainder of the lease term.

THE SYMMETRICAL REPAYMENT OF BORROWINGS

3.44 Consider first the position if the sterling and the dollar borrowings are paid off in a manner which is symmetrical with the receipt of the funds from which they are repaid.

In our over-simplified example, the only source from which funds are received is rentals: there are no receipts of "payments for group (tax) relief", or of interest on funds invested, until the very end of the lease term.

Therefore, by the end of the third quarter of year 3, the lessor will have received:-

	Rents received in sterling	Dollar rentals	(Sterling equivalent)
Eleven quarters @ £3,550	£39,050		
" " @ $7.100		$78.100	£39,050
He will have applied these in payment of interest	£13,761	$27,522	£13,761
in repayment of borrowing	£25,289	$50,578	£25,289

Thereafter, he will receive during the remaining nine quarters of the lease, further rentals as follows:-

Nine quarters @ £3,550	£31,950		
Nine quarters @ $7.100		$63,900	£35,500
and he will apply these			
in payment of interest	£ 2,870	$ 5,741	£ 3,189
in repayment of borrowing	£24,711	$49,422	£27,457
giving a balance, being surplus cash generated out of the lease	£ 4,369	$ 8,737	£ 4,854

3.45 The profits falling into each of the five years of the lease, using the investment period figures taken from paragraph 2.57 would be as follows:-

Year 1	–	**Sterling**		£1,108	
		Currency S2.215 @ S2.00		1,107	2,215
Year 2	–	**Sterling**		1,320	
		Currency $2.640 @ $2.00		1,320	2,640
Year 3	–	**Sterling**		990	
		Add Exchange difference arising on retranslating currency balances end year 2 at new rate of $1.80 in place of $2.00			
		Asset (net) $70,726	£ 3,929		
		Borrowing 65,164	(3,620)		
		Doubtful debts 707	(39)		
			270		
		Add profit for year $1,980 @ $1.80	1,100	1,370	2,360
Year 4	–	**Sterling**		611	
		Currency $1,221 @ $1.80		678	1,289
Year 5	–	**Sterling**		340	
		Currency $681 @ $1.80		379	719
		Total Sterling			£4,369
		Currency			4,854

The above method of laying out the figures has been adopted for purposes of clarity. The exchange surplus arising on restating a currency fixed asset at the new exchange rate would of course not normally be credited to income. If it were dealt with through reserves, the deficits on retranslating liabilities could be offset against it.

3.46 THE ASYMMETRICAL REPAYMENT OF BORROWINGS

On the other hand, if the lessor were to repay all of the dollar borrowing before starting to repay any sterling indebtedness, then his real profits would be wholly different. The pattern in which they fell into the years concerned would also change shape.

First eleven quarters

Rents received in currency		$ 78,100
Rents received in sterling	£39,050	
Utilised in paying sterling interest	13,761	
Utilised in repaying sterling borrowing	578	
	£24,711	
Converted into currency @ $2.00	£24,711	$ 49,422
		$127,522
Utilisation of currency—in paying interest		$ 27,522
—in repaying borrowing		$100,000

Final nine quarters

Outstanding sterling borrowing at end of eleventh quarter, after payment of £578 (as above)		£ 49,422
Rents received in sterling	£31,950	
Rents received in currency $63.900 converted into sterling @ $1.80	35,500	
	£67,450	
Utilised in paying interest	5,741	
	£61,709	
Utilised in repaying borrowing	49,422	£ 49,422
Surplus—representing profit over lease	£12,287	

The positive cash flow from this lease, when all the figures were sterling, was £8,737. It has become £12,287, an increase of £3,550. This increase is the extra sterling received from converting (not translating) $63,900 of rentals in the final nine quarters into sterling at an improved rate.

TERMINATION RENTAL VALUES

3.47 Increasingly often clauses are to be found in leases specifying the amount which the lessor would require from the lessee on a premature termination. The initiative for writing in these provisions comes from the lessee as frequently as it does from the lessor. Without them, the lessee might be liable at least in theory, to pay all the remaining rentals for the unexpired part of the lease period, should he wish to terminate the lease because of obsolescence or some other reason. This would be an unduly harsh penalty if it were to be applied. We have seen in paragraph 1.04 above that there is some doubt about the attitude the courts would take. Inserting a termination rental value into the lease is, however, one way in which the lessee can reduce the uncertainties of his position.

CALCULATING THE FIGURES

3.48 The calculation of the termination rental value is generally such as to ensure to the lessor, as a minimum, a rate of return, equal to that implicit in the lease.

In assuring himself of that rate of return, he will take into account the realisable value of the asset. He will also have regard to the effect that realisation will have on his tax calculations—by causing a recapture of allowances previously given. The formula under which the figure is to be arrived at can therefore be complex. As an alternative, but one which is not so frequently met in practice, the termination rental value may be specified as one of a series of monetary amounts laid down in the lease for different dates.

3.49 The underlying principles upon which the level of payments might be quantified can probably be seen most clearly if we ignore taxation and revert to the original data in paragraph 2.07.

We have seen in paragraph 2.43 that this really represents the figures for an annuity whose rate is 4.045% per quarter:

		Outstanding at beginning of quarter		Interest thereon paid at end of quarter	Capital repayment at end of quarter
Year 1	Q1	92,900		3,758	3,342
	Q2	89,558		3,623	3,477
	Q3	86,081		3,480	3,620
	Q4	82,461 →		← 3,335	3,765
Termination Rental Value			85,796		
Year 2	Q1	78,696		3,183	3,917
	Q2	74,779		3,025	4,075
	Q3	70,704		2,859	4,241
	Q4	66,463 →		← 2,688	4,412
Termination Rental Value			69,151		
....			and so on to	....	
Year 5	Q2	13,384		541	6,559
	Q3	6,825		275	6,825

The derivation of the termination rental value at the end of each year is self evident, but it does of course have to be stressed that this is an over-simplified illustration of the principles rather than a realistic calculation. In practice the lessor would take not only rental inflows into account, but also other inflows and outflows, tax being a major one of these.

TAKING THE FIGURES INTO ACCOUNT

3.50 The question then arises whether one should take account of termination values when one accounts for lease income.

If the asset were shown in the balance sheet at the end of year 1 at a figure equal to the termination payment at that point:-

Cost	£100,000
less depreciation	14,204
	£ 85,796

then it must follow that the gross income recognised in that year would be:-

Rent	£ 28,400
less depreciation	14,204
	£ 14,196

The aggregate of the "interest elements" of the first four instalments of the "annuity" comes to £14,196.

THE ARGUMENTS FOR USING TERMINATION RENTAL VALUES IN QUANTIFYING INCOME

3.51 The two arguments in favour of using termination rental values in quantifying income are that:

a) The termination rental value represents the most sophisticated application of the annuity method and is therefore the best measure at any one time of the income earned by the lessor to date, particularly where, as here, the lease is a very simple flow of rental income and nothing more;

b) if the lessor's rate of return is guaranteed at a minimum level by the existence of the termination clause, then surely this minimum level should be taken as the measure of profit.

THE ARGUMENTS AGAINST USING TERMINATION RENTAL VALUES IN QUANTIFYING INCOME

3.52 Those who argue against the use of these values in quantifying income to do on two main grounds, namely

a) that early terminations are exceptional—perhaps 2% or 3% of a normal leasing portfolio.
It is therefore incorrect to use such an unusual eventuality as the standard against which to measure the anticipated result of the other 97% or 98% of transactions;

b) that termination rental values are not explicitly set out in many leases. They have to be implied from the terms of the lease or from the assumptions inherent in the original rental calculation. This is not the most satisfactory basis for an accounting method.

3.53 Our view is that termination rental values are not, without supporting evidence, a sufficient basis upon which to formulate the lessor's basis of accounting. The proposition that, even when a value is not explicitly stated in a lease, it can nevertheless be assumed that there is such a value implicit therein, may possibly be true. But this does not mean that an implicit termination value can be relied upon, unaided, to measure truly and fairly the lessor's profit.

BUY-BACK CLAUSES

3.54 There is another form of termination arrangement, the principles of which are similar, but the effects different. Lessors frequently arrange with independent manufacturers to provide leasing facilities for their customers. Benefits flow to all three of the parties; the manufacturer finds it easier to increase his sales, the customer may find it a more convenient and economical way of obtaining the asset he needs and the finance company profits from helping the others.

3.55 The existence of a continuing relationship between manufacturer and lessor enables each to view his motivation in a rather different light, as compared to the way in which they would approach an isolated and unrelated deal. The manufacturer will frequently accept that he rather than the lessor should bear the risk of a bad debt occuring on a "sale" made through the lessor. He also, and more importantly from our point of view, accepts that he must retain the ultimate risks associated with the lessee's possible desire for an early termination.

3.56 The lessor therefore is allowed, in cases of early termination, to step out of his obligations, receiving from the manufacturer a lump sum which provides him the wherewithal to repay funds borrowed for investment in the lease, and provides him also his implicit rate of return. The manufacturer receives back his asset, and may or may not feel that he should additionally expect something further by way of compensation from the lessee.

3.57 What we are concerned with is the lump sum received by the lessor from the manufacturer. This part of the arrangement is usually known as a "buy-back clause", and the sum itself as a "buy-back price". The underlying principles on which it is calculated are similar to those for termination rental values. The lessor is to be guaranteed his rate of return on funds invested.

THE ACCOUNTING IMPLICATIONS

3.58 The accounting implications for the lessor are, in our view, distinguishable from those arising from termination rental values in that:-

a) Manufacturers make buy-back payments more often than lessees are called on to pay over termination rental values. This greater likelihood that he will be "bought out" is itself a factor which lends weight to the lessor's view of himself as a financier—see (b) and (c) below.

b) The lessor does not bear the risks of bad debts and is thus more firmly on the "purely financing" side of the fence than he is in unrelated leases;

c) To the extent that the lessor is more a financier, and less a vendor, he can properly say that his income should be quantified on purely financial principles. Assumptions about the length of the investment period and other similar matters therefore become less significant.

d) In an operating lease, the buy-back amount may be the only reliable guide to the amount of profit which has been earned.

In these cases it seems appropriate for a lessor to base his income release upon the existence of his buy-back prices. He is in a different position from the lessor who we suggested in paragraph 3.53 should not use termination rental values, alone, as his basis of accounting.

INTEREST RATE CHANGES

3.59 The data in Chapter 2 embodied a constant interest payable rate throughout the lease. This could be taken as an assumption that fixed rate finance was available to the lessor for the whole period. In practice lessors are often unable to, or do not choose to, match their book in this way, and their profits are thus susceptible to variations caused by interest rate changes. If we alter the cash flow figures previously set out in paragraph 2.08 we can show the effect of an increase at the end of year 2 in the rate of interest payable from 3½ per cent per quarter to 4 per cent per quarter, (from 14.75 per cent per annum to 17 per cent per annum). Interest receivable remains unchanged at 2½ per cent per quarter. The revised cash flow statement is set out in the appendix as Table A. It will be seen that the original pre-tax profit from the lease of £8,737 has been reduced by an additional borrowing cost of £2,012 to a figure of £6,525.

CHANGES IN THE PROFIT PATTERN

3.60 The effect of this change on the pattern of profit for the final three years of the lease can then be seen as follows:

	Year 1	Year 2	Year 3	Year 4	Year 5	Total
Straight Line						
Rent less depreciation	£ 8,400	£ 8,400	£ 8,400	£ 8,400	£ 8,400	£ 42,000
Interest	(12,178)	(9,786)	(8,113)	(4,666)	(732)	(35,475)
Doubtful debts	(800)	200	200	200	200	–
	(£4,578)	(£1,186)	£ 487	£ 3,934	£ 7,868	£ 6,525
Previously (Paragraph 2.09)	(4,578)	(1,186)	1,561	4,712	8,228	8,737
Annuity						
Rent less depreciation	14,196	11,755	8,894	5,542	1,613	42,000
Interest	(12,178)	(9,786)	(8,113)	(4,666)	(732)	(35,475)
	£ 1,160	£ 2,135	£ 977	£ 1,104	£ 1,149	£ 6,525
Previously (Paragraph 2.44)	1,160	2,135	2,051	1,882	1,509	8,737
Rule of 78						
Rent less depreciation	14,800	11,600	8,400	5,200	2,000	42,000
Interest	(12,178)	(9,786)	(8,113)	(4,666)	(732)	(35,475)
Doubtful Debts	(864)	168	200	232	264	–
	£ 1,758	£ 1,982	£ 487	£ 766	£ 1.532	£ 6,525
Previously (Paragraph 2.50)	1,758	1,982	1,561	1,544	1,892	8,737
Investment Period						
Rent	28,400	28,400	28,400	28,400	28,400	142,000
Depreciation	(13,138)	(16,136)	(19,810)	(23,459)	(27,457)	(100,000)
	15,262	12,264	8.590	4,941	943	42,000
Interest	(12,178)	(9,786)	(8,113)	(4,666)	(732)	(35,475)
Doubtful debts	(869)	162	198	234	275	–
	£ 2,215	£ 2,640	£ 675	£ 509	£ 486	£ 6,525
Previously (Paragraph 2.57)	£ 2,215	£ 2,640	£ 1,980	£ 1,221	£ 681	£ 8,737

3.61 Before going on to comment on these figures it is worth mentioning that the investment period calculations have themselves had to be revised. Because the period in which capital is still invested in the lease has been extended beyond the date previously anticipated, the gross income for which credit had not already been taken up to the end of year 2 has been re-spread through years 3, 4 and 5. the calculations are as follows:-

Year 1	**Q1**	£ 96,151			
	Q2	92,168			
	..... and so on		Giving	Year 1	£15,262
			Apportionment		
Year 2	Q3	70,060	of income	Year 2	12,264
	Q4	65,164		Sub total	£27,526
		£649,519			
Anticipated total to Year 5	Q2	£991,007			
Year 3	Q1	60,387			
	Q2	55,418	Giving	Year 3	8,590
			Apportionment		
	.....and so on		of income	Year 4	4,941
Year 5	Q2	7,805		Year 5	943
	Q3	734			
		£355,413		Sub total	£14,474

3.62 Going back to the changed pattern of profit resulting from a rise in the interest rate, we can say that there does not appear to be any great distortion of the patterns previously established under the straight-line method, the annuity method or the rule of 78. In each case the original figures themselves were open to some measure of criticism. The revised figures can be criticised for the same shortcomings, but do not appear to have created an entirely new degree of distortion. The investment period figures can similarly be defended as showing a fair pattern of profits in the altered circumstances.

3.63 **A MORE SIGNIFICANT CHANGE IN THE INTEREST RATE**
Distortion is, however, obviously a question of degree. We can further test the effects by making a more dramatic change in the interest rate. Let us assume that at the end of the second year the interest payable rate moves not to 4 per cent per quarter but to 4½ per cent per quarter. The cash flow statement then requires re-working once again, and this second revision is set out in the appendix as Table B. The original pre-tax profit from the lease of £8,737 has now been reduced by an additional borrowing cost of £4,594 to a figure of £4,143. Once again, the investment period itself alters, so that the apportionment of gross income to years 3, 4 and 5 alters, as shown in Table C in the appendix.

REVISED PROFIT PATTERNS

3.64 The patterns of pre-tax profit reported for the lease under each of the different methods now appear as follows:-

	Year 1	Year 2	Year 3	Year 4	Year 5	Total
Straight line						
Pre-tax line	(4,578)	(1,186)	(603)	3,092	7,418	4,143
Originally (Paragraph 2.09)	(4,578)	(1,186)	(1,561)	4,712	8,228	8,737
Annuity Method						
Pre-tax line	1,160	2,135	(113)	262	699	4,143
Originally (Paragraph 2.44)	1,160	2,135	2,051	1,882	1,509	8,737
Rule of 78						
Pre-tax line	1,758	1,982	(603)	(76)	1,082	4,143
Originally (Paragraph 2.50)	1,758	1,982	1,561	1,544	1,892	8,737
Investment Period						
Pre-tax line	2,215	2,640	(673)	(290)	251	4,143
Originally (Paragraph 2.57)	2,215	2,640	1,980	1,221	681	8,737

3.65 The comparisons set out in the preceding paragraph clearly show that the revised figures are very different from those originally calculated. So far as the straight line method, the annuity method and the rule of 78 are concerned, the way in which these differences fall into years 3, 4 and 5 appears to be purely arbitrary. It becomes impossible to defend the patterns of profits and losses now demonstrated under each of these methods even to the extent that they could previously have been regarded as acceptable. The only accounting system which comes out of this comparison with any degree of credit appears to be the investment period method. Distortion still exists but is much less than under the other methods.

CONCLUSIONS TO BE DRAWN

3.66 What can be deducted from these illustrations?

First, if we look again at the original pattern of profit through the five years of the lease, the amount by which this pattern has been distorted least is in the investment period method.

This can be explained as follows. When the interest rate changes, the aggregate profit over the five years falls to £4,143, this being a reduction of £4,594. This reduction comprises the higher interest charges in the final three years as follows:-

	Year 3	Year 4	Year 5	Total
Increased interest charge (from 3½% to 4½%)	£2,164	£1,620	£ 810	£4,594

It is reasonably clear that if these figures are deducted from a profit line which itself is sloping downwards through those three years, the result will be less distorted than it would be if the profit line were sloping upwards. We can see this as follows:-

	Year 3	Year 4	Year 5	Total
Investment period—(down sloping line)	£1,980	£1,121	£ 681	£3,882
Deduct	(2,164)	(1,620)	(810)	(4,594)
	(£ 184)	(£ 399)	(£ 129)	(£ 712)
Straight-line method—(upward sloping line)	£1,561	£4,712	£8,228	£14,501
Deduct	(2,164)	(1,620)	(810)	(4,594)
	(£ 603)	£3,092	£7,418	£9,907

3.67 But secondly, the investment period method enables us to recalculate the way in which income should be spread through the remainder of the lease term, after any change in the data on which the original spread was based. We can see the effect of this as follows:-

	Year 3	Year 4	Year 5	Total
Profit originally anticipated under investment period method	£1,980	£1,221	£ 681	£3,882
Deduct increased interest charge	(2,164)	(1,620)	(810)	(4,594)
	(184)	(399)	(129)	(712)
Reallocation resulting from recalculation of investment period	(489)	109	380	–
	(£ 673)	(£ 290)	£ 251	(£ 712)

It may not be easy to see that a "better" final line results using the figures set out above, but this ability to recalculate the way in which income is recognised can be expected to smooth rather than distort the end result. Each of the other methods is based on a "rent less depreciation" formula which is not responsive to change.

THE REINVESTMENT PROBLEM

3.68 It may not be a matter on which we can draw any conclusions, but it is also relevant that of the pre-tax profit of £251 recognised in the final year, an amount of £101 is derived in the last quarter of that year from reinvestment of surplus income. Many lessors regard this as a surplus that should be accounted for as it arises.

The argument runs that surplus income will normally have been invested in further leasing activities.

But, although the second lease, in which investment has been made, is taking the interest payable into its calculations of the investment period, that does not tell us what is the appropriate time for that same interest to be credited to the first lease. In any business which is not contracting, it is likely that surplus funds will be invested towards new business being written—interest receivable by the "investing lease" and payable by the "borrowing lease", being notional. But accounting theory does not yet tell us whether or not to account simultaneously for these notional receipts and payments.

LOSSES WHICH ARE FOLLOWED BY PROFITS

3.69 However, looking again at the figures in paragraph 3.67, there is another question which we can ask, but on which we will again find it hard to reach any conclusions. If the new source of finance is fixed at 4½% per quarter, the lessor might argue that a pattern of losses in the third and fourth years followed by profits in the last year is meaningless and therefore unacceptable. One possible method of dealing with this would be to spread back profits from the final year to years 3 and 4 but we cannot recommend this. The only basis upon which it would seem possible to do such a reallocation would be simply to reduce the final year's profit to zero. Neither that reduction, nor the way in which the £251 should be put into years 3 and 4, is a calculated adjustment. It makes little sense to base one's accounting method on complex calculations, and then to change the final result arbitrarily.

PROVIDING FOR LOSSES

3.70 There is also another point on which it is difficult to be dogmatic but on which we can offer some guidance. In our example using the investment period method we have seen that the 4½% per quarter interest payable for years 3, 4 and 5 produces a loss. This loss is shown in paragraph 3.67 at £712. Prudent accounting would require that this loss be provided for at the end of year 2. However, not providing at that point is precisely in line with the underlying principles of the investment period method. Many of the critics of this method regard this as a fallacy in the method. The same problem exists in all the accounting methods, but in the others it is normally masked by the income still to be taken to credit over the remaining period of the lease. Our considered opinion is that it is only possible to decide whether a loss needs to be provided for if you look at the whole leasing portfolio, not at individual leases in that portfolio. To the extent that the particular lease we have been considering is financed from internal sources, the 4½% per quarter rate cannot give rise to a real "loss". It is merely the mirror image of interest receivable on funds invested by some other lease. However, to the extent that our particular lease is funded from external sources, the 4½% interest payable is a genuine cost, and it is entirely possible that it can give rise to a genuine loss. It would be quite proper to make provision for such a loss at the end of year 2, if it is a part of a larger loss anticipated on the whole portfolio.

3.71 In practice, the whole question of whether there will or will not be a loss on a particular lease, or on the portfolio as a whole, is bound to be even more difficult as external interest rates, (on those funds not generated internally), are often not fixed for a particular period. The borrowing costs of the lessor will therefore vary, and so will his anticipation that profit or loss will result. More or less the only solution to this is the purely pragmatic one of evaluating the future pattern of income from each and every lease in the book at a given point, using the then prevailing rates of interest. If this calculation shows that for the whole portfolio of the company's leases, an overall loss is to be anticipated, provision for that loss anticipated by the company should be made immediately.

REMOVING THE UNCERTAINTIES

3.72 Assuming that the lessor has not borrowed funds at a fixed rate, and that he is therefore faced with uncertainty over future interest levels, how can he deal with this uncertainty? Two ways have emerged, one an accounting solution and the other a commerical solution. The accounting solution adopted by some lessors has been the use of an accounting method which is excessively "prudent" such for instance as the straight-line method. This tends to defer recognising income in such a way that even if interest rates move substantially, the additional costs can still be absorbed without the profit and loss account disclosing what has happened. The disadvantages of the straight-line method and of its application in this way, have already been pointed out.

INTEREST VARIATION CLAUSES

3.73 The commercial solution adopted by many lessors is to insert in their leases an "interest variation clause". These clauses trigger a variation in lease rentals following a variation in interest rates. They are not often popular with lessees because they destroy one of the advantages of lease finance, namely the certainty of the cost. Normally a lessor will be prepared to bear a certain percentage of any rise in interest rates, but he will want to increase rentals once that point has been reached. As a quid pro quo the lessee will expect a reduction in lease rentals if interest rates fall. The lessor will normally protect his position by specifying a minimum rate of interest below which no further lease rental adjustment is made.

3.74 If he fails to protect his interests in this way his suffering will be compounded. First, he will receive a reduced rental from the lessee. Secondly, he will earn a lower rate of interest on surplus funds, this factor being very important in a tax-based lease. If, as many lessors do, he has included an assumed rate of interest on surplus funds in his calculations of the lease rental, then he could be in trouble.

THE DRAFTING OF THE CLAUSE

3.75 The drafting of such clauses is not standard, but there are two basic forms in wide use. One specifies that if interest rates rise by X per cent, then lease rentals increase by Y per cent. This form is simple to understand and simple to operate. However it fails to take account of the level of the lessor's exposure. Increases in interest rates are costly in proportion to the amount of capital still invested. On a non-tax based lease, this exposure declines relatively evenly over the lease, and therefore one would expect the interest variation clause to reflect this. In a tax-based lease, the exposure usually exists only in the early part of a lease, so that a rise in interest rates which triggered an interest variation clause of the type referred to above in, say, the fourth year of a five year lease would give the lessor a bonus profit. A lessee might well argue that this was inequitable.

3.76 The lessee might accordingly ask the lessor to adopt the alternative form of interest variation clause, namely one that guarantees the lessor the same rate of return as envisaged in his original lease calculations. This is the more equitable way of dealing with the problem. But the wording of such clauses can be very complex, unless they merely require the lessor's auditor to certify what additional rentals are required from the lessee to protect the lessor's rate of return

3.77 The presence of an interest variation clause protects the lessor and enables him to overcome his accounting problem. Nevertheless, the increasing demand from lessees for fixed rate finance makes it likely that many leases will have to be written without such clauses. The lessor will need to assess his risks at each period end and provide for any anticipated loss. His decision may be largely subjective, but this seems vastly preferable to the alternative, namely adopting an overly conservative method of accounting

TAX CHANGES

3.78 A change in the rate of corporation tax is unlikely, in a non-tax based lease, to do more than reduce the post tax rate of return for the lessor. However, in a tax-based lease, the situation can be entirely different, arising from the timings of the receipt of tax relief and the payment of tax. If we assume that the figures in paragraph 2.71 are varied to illustrate the rate of taxation increasing from 52% to 55% for profits taxable in the third and subsequent years, then the cash flow will be as set out in Table D of the appendix.

TAX ADJUSTMENT CLAUSES

3.79 It is possible, once again, for the lessor to maintain his implicit rate of return by requiring the lessee to make higher payments of rent under a tax adjustment clause. The drafting of such clauses is just as complex an exercise as is that of the interest adjustment clauses referred to in paragraph 3.76. As with those clauses it is necessary to consider not only a rise in tax (or interest) which would reduce a lessor's rate of return, but also what should be the position if tax rates fall—to what extent should the benefit be given to the lessee?

PROTECTION AGAINST NON-AVAILABILITY OF FIRST YEAR ALLOWANCES

3.80 We should also mention that some lessors insist on a tax adjustment clause designed to protect their implicit rates of return should first year allowances on the leased assets be withheld or withdrawn.

WITHDRAWAL OF CASH FROM A LEASE

3.81 We indicated in paragraph 2.13 that one of the assumptions made for all illustrations in that part of Chapter 2 was that all cash not used in paying interest was used to reduce borrowings. Let us now explore what the effect would be if part of such cash was "withdrawn from the lease", for instance by way of payment of dividend.

3.82 Taking cash from one lease to use it in another is not quite the same thing. As no third party is involved, it can more accurately be seen as the investment by the first lease of its surplus funds, balanced by the borrowing for the second lease of those same funds. The accounting for the separate leases can properly show interest receivable for the first, and payable by the second—this item "washing" in the company's accounts. The only real difference from previous data is that there must be a specific identity of the rate at which interest is receivable and payable on this element of the financing of each lease.

WITHDRAWAL BY WAY OF DIVIDEND

3.83 To revert to the real withdrawal of cash from a lease by way of dividend, we can recalculate the cash flow figures previously set out in paragraph 2.08 to show an annual dividend of £1,000 paid at the end of each of years 1 to 4 inclusive. The figures are set out in the appendix as Table E. We have chosen to ignore tax, since the incidence of ACT on dividends is likely to distort the figures. It will be seen that the positive cash flow of £8,737 has been reduced to £3,096. The movement of £5,641 consists of £4,000 of dividends withdrawn from the lease and an additional interest cost of £1,641 on the revised amounts of borrowing needed to finance the lease.

3.84 If we now calculate income under the investment period method using these figures and using quarterly rests, the period itself and the apportionment of income within it are shown in Table F in the appendix.

PROFIT AND LOSS ACCOUNT USING THE INVESTMENT PERIOD METHOD

3.85 The profit and loss account for the lease then looks like this:

	Year 1	Year 2	Year 3	Year 4	Year 5	Total
Rent	£28,400	£28,400	£28,400	£28,400	£28,400	£142,000
Depreciation	(13,793)	(16,479)	(19,561)	(23,097)	(27,070)	(100,000)
	14,607	11,921	8,839	5,303	1,330	42,000
Interest Paid	(12,178)	(9,933)	(7,357)	(4,399)	(1,037)	(34,904)
	2,429	1,988	1,482	904	293	7,096
Doubtful Debts	(862)	165	195	231	271	–
	1,567	2,153	1,677	1,135	564	7,096
Dividend	(1,000)	(1,000)	(1,000)	(1,000)	–	(4,000)
	£ 567	£ 1,153	£ 677	£ 135	£ 564	£ 3,096

This compares with the figures for the investment period, non-tax based, lease as calculated in paragraph 2.57, where no provision is made for dividends:-

£ 2,215	£ 2,640	£ 1,980	£ 1,221	£ 681	£ 8,737

THE SHIFTING OF PROFITS

3.86 The calculations above naturally show a pre-dividend profit smaller than the profit calculated in paragraph 2.57. The pattern of profits, however, does approximate, although there is a noticeable shift of profit towards later years at the expense of the earlier years.

This shift results from the investment period, or pattern of exposure, having been extended further into those later years. It follows that it is extremely important when predicting the future pattern from a lease to use the correct parameters. In those accounting methods where interest is taken as it falls, the effect is significant. It is doubly significant in the investment period method, since it affects not only the impacting of interest itself into the profit and loss account, but also the period and pattern of recognition of gross income.

INTERNAL AND EXTERNAL FUNDING

3.87 One of the assumptions used throughout chapter 2 is that the lease is wholly financed by borrowed funds and that whether these are derived from internal or external sources, the interest payable rate to be used should be the same as that applicable to external borrowings. By external sources we mean borrowings from outside the company, whereas internal sources refer to the use of funds which are surplus to the needs of one lease, for investment in another. In practice some of the internally provided funds will be surplus cash from other leases and some will be shareholders funds. Under most of the methods of accounting this alters the profit levels without significantly changing the time at which profits are recognised, since interest impacts profit and loss account when it becomes payable. However, under the investment period method, interest costs affect also the level of capital invested, and the period of that investment.

3.88 Once again it is possible to vary the figures originally set out in paragraph 2.08 to demonstrate the effect of assuming a required rate of return on internal funds of 2% per quarter (8¼% per annum) and assuming that those internal funds are one quarter of the total. The revised cash flow is set out in Table G, and the apportionment of gross income through the investment period is recalculated in Table H.

EFFECTS ON THE PATTERN OF PROFIT

3.89 The investment period pre-tax profits work out as follows, and these figures are compared with the original pre-tax profits calculated on the assumption of an external interest rate of 3½% per quarter on all funds in paragraph 2.57:-

	Year 1	Year 2	Year 3	Year 4	Year 5	Total
Pre-tax profit assuming 2% interest on internal funds	£4,291	£4,225	£3,017	£1,651	£ 906	£14,090
Assuming 3½% on all funds	2,215	2,640	1,980	1,221	681	8,737

Since the profit level itself has varied, the profit pattern is easier to see if one re-states these two sets of figures in terms of cumulative percentages of total profit recognised at each year end, as follows:-

2% interest on internal funds	31%	60%	82%	94%	100%
3½% interest on all funds	25%	56%	78%	92%	100%

It can be seen that more of the gross income is pushed towards the beginning of the lease. This is one further underlining of the importance of the different assumptions which can be used as the basis of investment period calculations.

DETERMINING THE CORRECT COST OF FUNDS

3.90 The determination of the correct interest rate becomes more difficult where the lessor is a member of a group, and takes some or all of its finance requirements from another group company. One's initial reaction may be to say that whatever interest is charged to the lessor on group funds made available will on consolidation cancel out the interest receipt in the lending company and that intra group rate is therefore unimportant. This ignores the fact that each company is a separate legal entity. Apart from the obligation for each company to prepare its own separate accounts it is also necessary that each company is run in a way which does not totally disregard the interests of third parties—employees and creditors for example. The directors of the lessor are therefore under an obligation to make sure that the group rate charged to them is realistic.

3.91 In addition to its direct effect on the lessor's reported profits, the group interest rate will have an indirect effect on the timing of the profits where the investment period is in use. This is because it can alter the length of that investment period, which will accelerate or delay the recognition of profit.

3,92 Once the appropriate group cost of funds has been determined, there is no doubt that it must be used in the preparation of the statutory accounts of the lessor company which has been charged that rate, and also in the accounts of the group company which financed it.

But what about the consolidated accounts? The interest charge itself will "wash" on consolidation; however, there is a faultlessly logical and theoretical argument that the investment periods of each of the lessor's leases should be recalculated so as to reflect the consolidated cost of funds in place of the cost used by the lessor as a separate entity.

In practice such a reclaculation would be enormously laborious. For this reason, and because the benefit would be negligible, it simply is not done.

3.93 We have indicated the need for arriving at a group cost of funds, and also where and when it should be used. What we have not done is to indicate how to calculate it. This is not a treatise on banking. We therefore leave this problem unanswered, apart from saying that the rate should leave a margin of profit to the company providing the funds, as well as permitting the recipient of them to quote competitive terms for the leasing business which it offers. But theory is not easy to turn into practice. In a clearing bank—and each clearer has a substantial leasing company in its group—a single cost of funds is not only unobtainable, it is meaningless. Customers current balances cost nothing in terms of interest. Overnight funds in multiples of millions of pounds are expensive, but just how expensive, may well vary from minute to minute.

THE LESSOR'S AGGREGATE INTEREST EXPENSE

3.94 There is however a rather different point which arises in the general area of interest charged to lessor companies.

In all of our worked examples in this book so far we have looked at individual leases, and we have taken into our calculations a particular rate of interest payable for the cash invested in each lease.

In paragraphs 3.90 to 3.93 above we have turned our attention to something rather different, namely the total interest expense incurred by the lessor company for its whole portfolio.

3.95 Obviously lessors would aim at having the aggregate interest expense in each of their individual lease calculations equate to the total expense shown in their accounts. If they achieve this identity, it would be admirable, but it would also be surprising.

Rates payable (and receivable) on some funds will almost certainly have been greater than on others. These differences are impossible to mirror accurately in the individual lease calculations. Other differences may arise through such things as daily variations in overdraft rates, and the calculations of that interest charge on daily rather than on monthly or quarterly rests.

It is therefore highly likely that the company's accounts will reflect a different final profit level, (after the charging of the actual interest on the total borrowing), from the aggregate profits shown in the individual lease calculations. If the discrepancy is too great then there might possibly be a need to recalculate the income releases under the investment period method.

In normal circumstances, however, the lessor will have been able to estimate his interest expense as he incurs it—he will have made the individual lease calculations taking these expense levels into account. The discrepancy between these calculations and his accounts will be minimal, and his accounts will stand without any alteration.

STEP RENTALS AND BALLOON RENTALS

3.96 Intending lessees may wish in certain cases to negotiate leases in which the rents are not constant but rise regularly or irregularly through the term. In other cases they may wish the lease to require no rents for an initial period, but then provide for constant or rising rents thereafter.

These patterns of rents are known as step-rents. They are sometimes applied when rents can reasonably be related to production from the leased asset, and production is anticipated to build up during the term. They are also used when the finance provided by the lessor is to be used for construction of an asset and production cannot therefore commence until the asset has been completed.

3.97 Other leases may call for a substantial rental payment at the end of the lease term, the earlier payments being at a correspondingly lower level. This end-lease payment is known as a balloon rent.

MAINTAINING THE RATE OF RETURN

3.98 If the lessor is to preserve his same levels of profit as would arise under a constant-rent contract, it is clear that the rents themselves will need to be considerably greater.

We can illustrate this with the data from paragraph 2.07, varied to show an extreme position, namely no rents in any of the first four years, but increased rents in the final year. Using 3½% per quarter as the cost of funds, (equivalent to 14.75% per annum), the revised cash flow to produce an unchanged profit of £8,737 can be calculated as follows:-

		Rent receivable immediately before beginning of quarter	Outstanding borrowing at beginning of quarter or year	Interest payable (receivable) at end of quarter or year	Outstanding borrowing at end of quarter or year
Year 1		–	£100,000	£14,750	£114,750
Year 2		–	114,750	£16,926	131,676
Year 3		–	131,676	£19,422	151,098
Year 4		–	151,098	£22,287	173,385
Year 5	Q1	£47,630	125,755	4,401	130,156
	Q2	47,630	82,526	2,888	85,414
	Q3	47,630	37,784	1,323	39,107
	Q4	47,630	(8,523)	(214)	(8,737)
				8,398	
			Total	£81,783	

ACCOUNTING USING THE RULE OF 78 METHOD

3.99 Does the lessor need some special method to use in accounting for such an unusual pattern of rents?

We can best answer this by working the figures under one of our existing methods—in the first instance we will use the rule of 78:-

	Year 1	Year 2	Year 3	Year 4	Year 5	Total
Rents	–	–	–	–	£190,520	£190,520
Depreciation	£31,898	£25,001	£18,104	£11,207	(186,210)	(100,000)
	31,898	25,001	18,104	11,207	4,310	90,520
Interest	(14,750)	(16,926)	(19,422)	(22,287)	(8,398)	(81,783)
	17,148	8,075	(1,318)	(11,080)	(4,088)	8,737
Doubtful debts	(1,319)	(250)	(181)	(112)	1,862	–
	£15,829	£ 7,825	£ (1,499)	£(11,192)	£ (2,226)	£ 8,737

What we have done is simply to construct a gross income line, (rents less depreciation), in which the five years' figures are in the ratios of 74: 58: 42: 26: 10, these numbers being the "sums of the quarterly digits". But the final profit line is pure nonsense and shows that the rule of 78 cannot cope adequately with as extreme a rental pattern as this.

ACCOUNTING USING THE INVESTMENT PERIOD METHOD

3.100 However, when we try the investment period method, the result comes out as follows:-

	Year 1	Year 2	Year 3	Year 4	Year 5	Total
Rents	—	—	—	—	£190,520	£190,520
Depreciation	£16,283	£18,684	£21,441	£24,604	(181,012)	(100,000)
	16,283	18,684	21,441	24,604	9,508	90,520
Interest	(14,750)	(16,926)	(19,422)	(22,287)	(8,398)	(81,783)
	1,533	1,758	2,019	2,317	1,110	8,737
Doubtful debts	(1,162)	(188)	(214)	(246)	1,810	—
	£ 371	£ 1,570	£ 1,805	£ 2,071	£ 2,920	£ 8,737
Balance sheet at end of year						
Asset Amount	£100,000	£100,000	£100,000	£100,000	—	
Debtor	16,283	34,967	56,408	81,012	—	
	£116,283	£134,967	£156,408	£181,012	—	

The major part of the income is recognised towards the later years—the years in which risk and investment have built up to their greatest levels.

NEGATIVE DEPRECIATION

3.101 The gross income line, (rents less depreciation), now reflects the investment in the lease at each quarterly rest, but it is important to understand how this line has been constructed. It has been necessary to write in a "negative depreciation" figure in each of the first four years, in order to compensate for the absence of rent. In the fifth year, with a very heavy rental payment, the depreciation charge not only writes the asset down to zero, but reverses the previous years' negatives. It is not good practice to write up the value of the fixed asset itself by the amounts of negative depreciation. They are therefore shown as building up a separate asset, to be included in the balance sheet as a debtor.

SPREAD RENTS

3.102 Negative depreciation is not a universally acclaimed accounting concept. One way of avoiding it would be to frame the profit and loss account as if rents were receivable at a constant level through all the years.

	Year 1	Year 2	Year 3	Year 4	Year 5	Total
Rent	£38,104	£38,104	£38,104	£38,104	£38,104	£190,520
Depreciation	(21,821)	(19,420)	(16,663)	(13,500)	(28,596)	(100,000)
	16,283	18,684	21,441	24,604	9,508	90,520
	....	then as before	....			
	£ 371	£ 1,570	£ 1,805	£ 2,071	£ 2,920	£ 8,737
Balance sheet at end of year						
Asset amount	78,179	58,759	42,096	28,596	–	
Debtor	38,104	76,208	114,312	152,416	–	
	£116,283	£134,967	£156,408	£181,012	–	

A glance at the aggregate of the asset figures shows, unsurprisingly, that there has been no change from the aggreates in paragraph 3.100.

Depreciating the asset positively by building up a rental debtor is merely cosmetic, but many people find it more acceptable than the answer given in paragraph 3.100.

3.103 This method of taking profit before rent has been recieved, whether as presented in the manner shown in paragraph 3.100 or as in paragraph 3.102, has its critics, because of the dangers of bad debts. We believe that this is unjustified because the bad debt risk can be analysed, assessed and provided for in the correct place. In any event no lessor would be likely to grant such a rental pattern to any lessee whose financial standing was in the slightest doubt.

THE TREATMENT OF INITIAL DIRECT COSTS

3.104 The lessor's costs in setting up each of his leases may vary from lease to lease, and will certainly depend upon the type of business he writes. These initial direct costs will comprise commissions, salesmen's salary and expenses and a proportion of general administration expenses.

NO SPECIAL TREATMENT

3.105 One method of treating these costs is simply to do nothing and let them be charged to profit and loss account as and when they are incurred. For this to produce an acceptable result, it is necessary that the costs be relatively static, that their total amount is relatively smooth from period to period and that the business being written by the company is neither rapidly expanding nor contracting. Provided these conditions are met, as they may well be in a retail business whose lease contracts tend to be standard, then to do nothing should produce the right result.

3.106 To do nothing and to let initial direct costs hit the profit and loss account as they are incurred, means that today's costs are always being "matched" against the income generated by yesterday's costs. This produces the right answer only if neither costs nor income fluctuate. Therefore, unless the situation is as above, expenditure should not be written off immediately, but carried forward to be set against the income related to it. There is an exception if it is anticipated that the transaction will not be profitable overall.

Under the matching concept it is wrong to allow initial direct costs to fall into the first year of a lease in such a way as to cause a loss to appear, if the lease is profitable overall. It is also wrong to put initial direct costs into the first year if by doing so you deflate that year's profits, and thus disrupt or destroy the relationships between each year's profits throughout the lease.

THE MORE ACCEPTABLE METHODS

3.107 There are three methods available to produce a more acceptable answer. Each is capable of showing a meaningful trend of profits when business is expanding or contracting as well as when it is static. Each is also capable of coping adequately with uneven cost levels as well as smooth ones.

3.108 The first method requires an amount of income equal to the initial direct cost of each lease to be released in the period in which that cost was incurred. This means that there is no immediate impact on profit and loss account for costs at the time they are incurred, but the income available to be released during the lease term is correspondingly less. This smaller sum is recognised over the years of the lease under one or other of the accounting methods already examined.

3.109 The second method is a variation of the above. Under this method the total of the initial direct costs for a year are estimated, and the proportion deemed to relate to each lease is arrived at by dividing that total by the number of leases. Initial income release, and calculation of subsequent releases, then follow as before.

3.110 The third method is for the initial income release to be calculated simply as a percentage of gross income receivable on the lease concerned. In this case it is clearly necessary to check at regular intervals that the initial direct costs actually being incurred do still represent the appropriate percentage of gross income—and if not, to revise the percentage.

OTHER PROBLEMS OF THE INVESTMENT PERIOD METHOD

3.111 The figure spread by the investment period method is the gross income figure. The period over which it is spread is the time during which the lessor has an investment in the lease. Interest as it becomes due for payment is charged against the gross income. Credit is taken for interest on surplus funds as this interest becomes receivable.

The following restatement of the relevant figures from the tax-based investment period example in paragraph 2.80 highlights three specific points:-

	Year 1	Year 2	Year 3	Year 4	Year 5	Total
Rent less depreciation	£24,113	£16,355	£ 1,532	–	–	£42,000
Interest paid	(12,178)	(8,261)	(774)	–	–	(21,213)
received			14	1,160	2,711	3,885
	£11,935	£ 8,094	£ 772	£ 1,160	£ 2,711	£24,672

3.112 These three questions are first how rational is it to deal with interest receivable in the way in which it is handled above. If it is a fact that the lessor takes into account in his implicit rate calculations the interest he can generate from his positive cash flow, should that not be reflected in a similar way in his calculation of profits to be recognised?

Secondly, exactly how long is the investment period—if cash invested swings from positive to negative and back, does the period end when that dividing line is first crossed or only when the lessor has finally paid off his indebtedness.

Thirdly, there is a much wider question. If there is uncertainty about future interest rates, or about tax rates, or about the availability of first year allowances themselves, how can one work out what the investment period is likely to be?

3.113 As regards the first two questions in the preceding paragraph, neither has a conclusive answer. Arguments can be made out for and against each possibility, but in practice

a) Lessors usually credit their interest income as it arises. (As we have seen earlier, interest often "arises" as a reduction in the actual finance costs of another lease, rather than as a cash receipt),

and

b) They usually treat the investment period as ending at the latest of the possible dates.

Each of these practices is the more conservative of the alternatives, and is the one we recommend.

The only short answer to be given to the third question is that one must make the best estimate possible in the circumstances, erring on the side of prudence if the matter is in great doubt. We will return briefly to this matter in paragraph 5.02 below.

TAX LIABILITIES AND THE INVESTMENT PERIOD

3.114 There is a very good argument which says that, in deciding when the "investment" in the lease has come to an end, one must have regard not only to one's borrowings from the person who has provided normal finance, but also to ones "borrowings" from the Inland Revenue.

What is at issue can be seen most clearly if we take up the figures from the tax based cash flow statement in paragraph 2.71, but adjust them to recognise that the whole of the "tax recovery" in the fourth quarter of Year 2, £43,565, has to be "repaid" to the Revenue in the fourth quarters of Years 3, 4, 5 and 6. (The last mentioned repayment amounts to £3,349—the total payment to the Revenue at that point is £16,178, and the difference of £12,829 is the tax attributable to the lease profit of £24,672).

3.115 The outstanding borrowings at the ends of each quarter from the fourth quarter of year 2 are therefore as follows:-

		Outstanding borrowings previously	Tax (recovery) cumulative		Adjusted outstanding borrowings
Year 2	Q4	£20.074	£43,565		£63,639
Year 3	Q1	13,428	43,565		56,993
	Q2	6,550	43,565		50,115
	Q3	(564)	43,565		43,001
	Q4	2,906	33,093	(being 43,565	35,999
Year 4	Q1	(4,299)	33,093	less 10,472)	28,794
	Q2	(11,684)	33,093		21,409
	Q3	(19,254)	33,093		13,839
	Q4	(12,281)	18,720	(being 33,093	6,439
Year 5	Q1	(19,866)	18,720	less 14,373)	(1,146)
	Q2	(27,640)	18,720		(8,920)
	Q3	(35,609)	18,720		(16,889)
	Q4	(28,021)	3,349	(being 18,720 less 15,371)	(24,672)

This demonstrates that the lease still has cash "invested" in it until the end of the fourth year, rather than until the end of the third. On this basis a good case can be made for recognising that the investment period does not come to its close until the end of the fourth year. The pattern of income release would therefore not be what it has been shown to be in paragraph 2.80. But, although this modification of the investment period calculations is rational, it is not one which is commonly met in practice.

INCOME WHICH EXCEEDS RENTS

3.116 It is entirely possible that the investment period calculations will make the income to be recognised in the first period and beyond exceed the rent receipts.

The lessor has a choice between

a) Bending the results of these calculations, by recognising income only up to the level of rent received. The excess is then recognised in the next year—subject again to the limitation.

b) Recognising income at the level suggested, by charging "negative depreciation"—that is to say writing up the asset.

c) Creating a receivable in his balance sheet to the extent of the excess of recognisable income over rents, which is the answer we recommend.

CHAPTER 4 – THE LESSEE'S ACCOUNTS

Contents

INTRODUCTION

4.01 In this chapter we look at the accounts of the lessee.

The lessee has possession and use of the asset. He does not have, and is unlikely to get, legal title to the asset. But to a greater or lesser extent he enjoys at least some of the economic benefits. In the case of an operating lease, his possession and use may be only for part of the anticipated useful life of the asset, whereas in a finance lease he may well enjoy its whole effective life, and he may also participate to a substantial extent in its eventual disposal proceeds.

THE THREE ACCOUNTING METHODS

4.02 Assuming that there are no financial transactions apart from rental payments, the lessee can account for this possession and use in three possible ways:-

a) He can charge the rents to profit and loss account as they accrue;

b) He can charge amounts in the early years of the lease which exceed the rents actually payable (showing the excess as "deferred revenue" in his balance sheet). He would then charge amounts less than the rents actually payable in the later years. This treatment compensates in the profit and loss account for the fact mentioned in paragraphs 1.11 and 1.12 (and considered again in its accounting context in paragraph 2.33), namely that the advantages of leasing are a better cash flow and a lower level of expense in the early years of the lease than would be expected from full ownership.

c) In addition to charging the rents as in (b) above he can also show the asset itself in his balance sheet and show a liability figure for rentals due to the lessor in the future.

Where the lessee regards the transaction as an operating lease, (a) above is the correct treatment; there is little disagreement about this. Where the lessee is dealing with a finance lease, his options are wide open. We shall be examining, in paragraphs 4.08 to 4.24, the implications of each of the possible accounting methods available to him, and the criteria he should use in making his choice. But first he needs to decide if his lease is operating or finance. Whether this classification should mirror that of the lessor is a matter of contention, although, as we shall see in chapter 6, the U.S. Financial Accounting Standards Board is attempting to ensure that it should.

DISTINGUISHING FINANCE AND OPERATING LEASES

4.03 As this stage we need to remind ourselves of the distinction between finance and operating leases.

We defined the latter, in paragraph 1.03, as having the following characteristics:-

a) the profit which emerges to the lessor depends to a significant extent upon the lease-end asset value.

b) the lease term covers only a part of the anticipated useful life of the asset.

c) the lessor is usually responsible for maintenance and insurance of the leased asset.

d) the lease agreement may require the lessor to accept back the leased asset prematurely without a major penalty being imposed upon the lessee.

Finance leases we defined as the antithesis of the above.

We are now looking at the leases from the lessee's point of view, It may be more difficult for him to obtain the information he needs on which to make the necessary judgements—particularly in relation to (a) and (b) above. But this does not affect the validity of these tests as the ones which should be applied to distinguish finance leases from operating ones.

ACCOUNTING FOR OPERATING LEASES

4.04 If the lessee can properly regard the transaction as an operating lease, the correct accounting treatment is to charge the rentals as they fall due, method (a) in paragraph 4.02:-

Year 1	**Expense**	£28,400
2		28,400
3		28,400
4		28,400
5		28,400

The lessee should not capitalise any amount in his balance sheet, as this would imply that his interest (in the legal sense of that word) in the asset was nearer to ownership than to the possession and use obtained under an operating lease. Nor should he show any indebtedness, either current or prospective, for rent which has not yet fallen due.

4.05 This means not only that he should not treat all future rentals as being current or long term liabilites. It also means that the lessee should not follow the course outlined in paragraph 4.02 (b) of charging more than the actual rent in the lease's early years, and less in the later.

If the lessee had purchased the asset himself, the aggregate of his finance costs and depreciation charge in the early years would probably be greater than he would otherwise have paid in those early years by way of rent. But this is not the set of circumstances for which the lessee should be accounting. He has only a temporary and limited possession and use. Financing costs associated with ownership are irrelevant so far as he is concerned, except in the totally different context of the lessor's purchasing power, i.e. if the lessor by virtue of financial muscle can borrow more cheaply than others, can take advantage of bulk purchasing discounts or favourable prices and can obtain advantage from present fiscal legislation, then the lessee might hope to have some of these advantages passed on in the lease terms. Apart from this considera- tion he is not interested in the level of the lessor's yearly interest charge for the investment in the lease.

4.06 It is unlikely that the lessee will ever obtain legal title to the leased asset. He would not normally participate in any proceeds from its eventual disposal. In many, if not all cases, the lessor would expect to re-lease the asset rather than to sell it, because the lease

term bears no necessary relationship to the asset's useful life. Therefore the end of the lease term does not imply the end of the asset's worth.

In addition the lessor normally bears the insurance and maintenance costs. If these latter rise with the asset's age, that is no argument for the lessee to "compensate" by misstating his rental expense; the maintenance costs do not touch him.

All these points confirm that an operating lessee's possession and use is very far from having the full economic benefits and risks of ownership. We therefore repeat that the lessee's correct accounting treatment is to charge rents as they fall due.

DISCLOSURE REQUIRED BY SCH. 2(12)(1) COMPANIES ACT 1967

4.07 Disclosure is required in companies' accounts of the total paid in the period for items leased. This requirement of Sch. 2(12)(1) Companies Act 1967 is of course only a minimum disclosure and, in our view, is inadequate. One factual item, unrelated and out of context, could give a totally wrong impression to the reader of the accounts and it is not impossible that the view given by the accounts as a whole might cease to be true and fair. The disclosure of the rents paid in the year under operating leases should be supp- lemented in our view by a statement showing the amounts anticipated as due to be paid in each of the succeeding five years, and total anticipated thereafter. (We are dealing here only with disclosure of operating lease rentals; for finance lease rentals please refer to paragraph 4.25 below).

ACCOUNTING FOR FINANCE LEASES

4.08 Accounting for finance leases is not nearly so simple. Assuming that it is possible to identify finance leases, their correct accounting treatment is highly debatable. One method is to follow the treatment suggested in paragraph 4.02 (a) and outlined above i.e. do nothing and let the rents hit the profit and loss account as they fall due. But this method suffers from the same major defects as did the straight-line and market value methods used by some lessors to account for finance leases, (see paragraphs 2.31–2.34).

It fails to tackle the fundamental subject of matching. We saw in chapters 2 and 3 the lessor examining how best to match his expenditure against the rentals which form his income. What we now need to consider is the lessee's matching of those same rentals (expenditure so far as he is concerned) against his own income. The methods he can use to account for finance leases which do make matching possible are based on paragraph 4.02 (b), and take three forms:-

a) Mirror image capitalisation;

b) Discounted value capitalisation;

c) Profit and loss tapering.

The first two of these bring the asset into the balance sheet (see paragraph 4.02 (c))—the third does not.

MIRROR IMAGE CAPITALISATION

4.09 The first method we examine is described as mirror-image capitalisation.

For the sake of simplicity we will assume that the rental is £28,400 payable annually in arrear. The lessee is aware that the rate of interest implicit in the lessor's calculations is 12.95% per annum and he knows that his annual rent is £28,400. From this he calculates the following "annuity" table:

	Capital Outstanding	Annual Instalment Interest	Annual Instalment Capital
Year 1	£100,000	£12,955	£ 15,445
Year 2	84,555	10,954	17,446
Year 3	67,109	8,694	19,706
Year 4	47,403	6,141	22,259
Year 5	25,144	3,256	25,144
		£42,000	£100,000

4.10 The lessee next considers what depreciation policy would be appropriate. What he should be aiming at is:-

a) writing the asset down to its residual value at the end of its useful life. We can define that end as the point when repair and overhaul costs become prohibitive, or when obsolescence of asset or product render further operations pointless. Useful life should not be longer than the primary period of the lease. For illustration purposes we can assume a life of five years and a nil value at the end.

b) achieving a spread through the asset's useful life of the total costs associated with its possession and use—that spread to be related to the asset's earning capacity. This objective should be recognised as an extension of the fundamental accounting concept of matching costs with revenue.

Taking account of anticipated repairs and maintenance costs through the asset's life, the lessee may well come to the conclusion that his depreciation policy should be straight-line.

4.11 On the basis of these calculations and decisions, the lessee capitalises the asset in his books at the commencement of the lease at £100,000, the same figure as the "capital" of the annuity. He reflects this same figure on the other side of his balance sheet as indebtedness to the lessor.

4.12 The accounts then show, during the lease term

	Profit & Loss	Liability	Fixed asset
Commencement	–	£100,000	£100,000
Year 1 – Depreciation	20,000	–	20,000
"Interest"	12,955	12,955	–
	–	112,955	–
Cash Paid	–	28,400	–
End Year 1	£ 32,955	£ 84,555	£ 80,000
Year 2 – Depreciation	20,000	–	20,000
"Interest"	10,954	10,954	–
	–	95,509	–
Cash paid	–	28,400	–
End Year 2	£ 30,954	£ 67,109	£ 60,000
Year 3 – Depreciation	20,000	–	20,000
"Interest"	8,694	8,694	–
	–	75,803	–
Cash paid	–	28,400	–
End Year 3	£ 28,694	£ 47,403	£ 40,000
Year 4 – Depreciation	20,000	–	20,000
"Interest"	6,141	6,141	–
	–	53,544	–
Cash paid	–	28,400	–
End Year 4	£ 26,141	£ 25,144	£ 20,000
Year 5 – Depreciation	20,000	–	20,000
"Interest"	3,256	3,256	–
	–	28,400	–
Cash paid	–	28,400	–
End Year 5	£ 23,256	–	–
Total	£142,000		

Note that the asset and liability amounts will not remain equal after the lease commences.

4.13 We do need to appreciate the meaning of the phrase "mirror image capitalisation". What is indicated is that the basis upon which the lessee capitalises the asset is the same as that used by the lessor in his books. It does not mean that the assets and liabilities in the two sets of books are equal and opposite. There is for instance no receivable in the lessor's balance sheet which mirrors the liability to him which the lessee shows in his own.

Taking the straight-line, non-tax based, figures set out for the lessor in paragraph 2.09, we can compare his balance sheets at commencement, and one and two years on, with those of the lessee derived from paragraph 4.12. (For the latter we need to show the source from which the lessee found the cash to pay the rents—we show this cash coming from drawing on an overdraft).

LESSOR				LESSEE			
Commencement				**Commencmen**t			
Loan finance	£100,000	**Asset**	£100,000	**Lessor**	£100,000	**Asset**	£100,000
End of year 1				**End of year 1**			
Profit & loss	(4,578)	**Asset**	80,000	**Profit & loss**	(32,955)	**Asset**	80,000
Loan finance	83,778			**Lessor**	84,555		
Doubtful debts	800			**Overdraft**	28,400		
	£ 80,000		£ 80,000		£ 80,000		£ 80,000
End of year 2				**End of year 2**			
Profit & loss	(5,764)	**Asset**	60,000	**Profit & loss**	(63,909)	**Asset**	60,000
Loan finance	65,164			**Lessor**	67,109		
Doubtful debts	600			**Overdraft**	56,800		
	£ 60,000		£ 60,000		£ 60,000		£ 60,000

Because each is using a straight-line depreciation policy, the asset is stated at the same amounts but no other figures mirror each other. Whether the lessor's asset is a fixed asset or a debtor is a question already dealt with in paragraph 2.97 above.

DISCOUNTED VALUE CAPITALISATION

4.14 The second method is known as discounted value capitalisation. The lessee knows that if he borrowed money himself, he would be charged 15% interest. He can therefore calculate that annual instalments of £28,400 would cover interest and repayment of a loan of £95,201:-

	Capital outstanding	Annual instalment Interest	Capital
Year 1	£95,201	£14,280	£14,120
Year 2	81,081	12,162	16,238
Year 3	64,843	9,727	18,673
Year 4	46,170	6,926	21,474
Year 5	24,696	3,704	24,696

4.15 He can be fairly certain that the rate implicit in the lease is lower than 15%. He may know what it is, but even if he does not, he can confidently expect that the lessor would, in a tax based lease, have passed on to him some part of the advantage gained from the first year allowances.

The lessee argues that the true view of the situation is that he has been enabled to obtain, through leasing, an asset at a cheaper price, but at the interest rate which would normally have been charged, 15%. He says that it is untrue and unfair to say that he has "borrowed" the full price of the asset, even though the lease terms are based on a rate of interest on the borrowing lower than any normal lender would require.

In this way, the lessee contends that £95,201 is an entirely reasonable figure to capitalise in his books, even if it is not what the lessor paid for the asset.

4.16 The entries in the lessee's accounts then appear as follows, again assuming straightline depreciation.

		Profit and loss	Liability	Asset
	Commencement	–	£95,201	£95,201
Year 1	**Depreciation**	£19,041	–	19,041
	"Interest"	14,280	14,280	–
		–	109,481	–
	Cash paid	–	28,400	–
	End Year 1	£33,321	£81,081	£76,160
Year 2	**Depreciation**	19,040	–	19,040
	"Interest"	12,162	12,162	–
		–	93,243	–
	Cash paid	–	28,400	–
	End Year 2	31,202	64,843	57,120
Year 3	**Depreciation**	19,040	–	19,040
	"Interest"	9,727	9,727	–
		–	74,570	–
	Cash paid	–	28,400	–
	End Year 3	£28,767	£46,170	£38,080
Year 4	**Depreciation**	19,040	–	19,040
	"Interest"	6,926	6,926	–
		–	53,096	–
	Cash paid	–	28,400	–
	End year 4	£25,966	£24,696	£19,040
Year 5	**Depreciation**	19,040	–	19,040
	"Interest"	3,704	3,704	–
		–	28,400	–
	Cash paid	–	28,400	–
	End Year 5	£22,744	£ –	–

The lessee's asset and liability are shown at lower figures, not only initially, but at all subsequent stages, compared to the first method illustrated in paragraph 4.12 above. But just as important, and defended by the lessee as also being truer and fairer, is the heavy weighting of the profit and loss charge in the early years, and its tapering off more sharply thereafter.

PROFIT AND LOSS ACCOUNT TAPERING

4.17 The third method is not commonly encountered. The lessee makes the same annuity calculations we have just looked at, and adjusts his profit and loss charge to the figures indicated. He does not, however, show an asset in his balance sheet. Using the same annuity calculations as in paragraph 4.13, the entries in his accounts are as follows:-

		Profit and Loss	"Deferred Revenue" in Balance Sheet	
Year 1	Cash paid	£28,400		
	Balancing item	4,921	4,921	
	End Year 1	£33,321	£ 4,921	CR
Year 2	Cash paid	28,400		
	Balancing item	2,802	2,802	
	End Year 2	31,202	7,723	CR
Year 3	Cash paid	28,400		
	Balancing item	367	367	
	End Year 3	28,767	8,090	CR
Year 4	Cash paid	28,400		
	Balancing item	(2,434)	(2.434)	
	End Year 4	25,966	5,656	CR
Year 5	Cash paid	28,400		
	Balancing item	(5,656)	(5,656)	
	End Year 5	22,744	–	

The arguments for and against capitalisation and tapering are summarised below.

THE ARGUMENTS AGAINST CAPITALISATION

4.18 Capitalisation does not reflect the true legal position and this can cause problems. For instance, what effect does it have on borrowing limits set by the Articles of Association or by a Debenture Trust Deed if a company shows in its balance sheet a "borrowing" which in law is no such thing?

4.19 Capitalisation can cause distortions. For instance, as the Inland Revenue will only allow a deduction for the rents actually due, and not for some inflated profit and loss charge, the tax rate will appear abnormally high in the early years. One may not be able to deal with this by operating a deferred tax provision in the lessee's accounts. If this recognition of accounts profits later than taxable profits is the only "timing difference" in the accounts, then the deferred tax account necessary to compensate for it would have a debit balance—and would therefore appear as an asset in the balance sheet. This is not normally an acceptable accounting phenomenon. Therefore only if this "timing difference" can be netted off against others which operate in the reverse direction can a deferred tax provision help to remove this distortion.

4.20 Capitalisation by a lessee may create its own tax problems. How certain are we, for instance, that the lessor's position is totally unchanged in relation to his entitlement to capital allowances on "his" asset, if the lessee shows that he thinks it should be shown as not being the lessor's? Or how certain are we that the lessee will be entitled to deduct a rent which he does not appear to be charging in arriving at his accounting profits? We will return to these questions in chapter 5, but we must recognise at this point that the questions exist.

4.21 There is no dispute that in "form" a leasing transaction is one in which the asset remains the property of the lessor, and the lessee should not therefore pretend that it is his. In "substance" we have indicated that, so far as finance leases are concerned, the underlying reality is different. The rights and risks attaching to possession and use under a finance lease are so great, and those retained by the lessor representing his ownership are so much less material, that possession and use can be looked at as if it were ownership. But even in a lease which is indisputably finance rather than operating, the asset is still the lessor's. The lessee has some rights, but his obligations from a financial point of view are purely those of paying the rent.

THE ARGUMENTS FOR CAPITALISATION

4.22 It is a requirement of the Companies Acts that accounts should show a true and fair view, even if this conflicts with the legal form of a transaction or transactions. This has also been codified in International Accounting Standard No. 1 which states that substance should be accounted for rather than form. The principle has recently been reaffirmed by the Institute of Chartered Accountants in England and Wales in its guidance on showing inventories in a company's balance sheet even though the legal title to the goods concerned may have been reserved by the supplier in the manner allowed by the court in the Romalpa case. Similarly, inflation accounting, when finally introduced, will require companies to quantify profits in a manner which might bear no relation to the actual legal position. Thus, in our view, the fact that legally the asset subject to a finance lease belongs to the lessor is no argument against capitalisation by the lessee.

4.23 Tax distortions likewise should not be used as an argument against capitalisation. Taxable profits and tax liabilities do not, and need not bear any relationship to accounting profit. The companies acts specifically recognise this; what they require is not that tax charges be lined up with profit, (still less that profit be lined up with tax charges), but that disclosures be made by way of note of "any special circumstances which affect liability in respect of taxation of profits ..... for the financial year ..... or for future years", (Sch. 2(14)(3A) Companies Act 1967.)

Distortions should be disclosed, not adjusted and hidden.

THE AUTHORS' VIEW

4.24 The real question is that of substance.

Those who argue against capitalisation use as a main plank in that argument that the form of the transaction does not permit the lessee to put the asset into his balance sheet as if it is his own. They go on to say that neither does substance support that treatment.

We hear what they say, but we are not convinced. In our view substance is clearly different from form in a finance lease. The lessee enjoys virtually all the rewards, responsibilities and risks of ownership, without having legal title. The lessor has that title, but his own rights are heavily restricted (except when the lessee defaults on his obligations, and then the lessor's rights are akin to those of a creditor who holds security for his debt).

This view of the substance of the transaction certainly coincides with the lessor's attitudes. He regards it as one in which he appears as a financier. We have seen that he frequently tries to ensure that the lessee sees him in that light—the lessee has to accept adjustment clauses (for interest, tax and currency) designed to protect the lessor from the risks of ownership, and to limit his exposure to that of a lender.

Our view is that lessees should reflect this substance by capitalising the assets whose possession and use they acquire under finance leases.

DISCLOSURE REQUIRED BY Sch. 2(12)(1) COMPANIES ACT 1967

4.25 The Companies Acts disclosure requirements also apply to the lessee who capitalises the leased asset. What the 1967 Act requires is that the profit and loss account should show:-

> "the amount if material, charged to revenue in respect of sums payable in respect of the hire of plant and machinery".

In the example in paragraph 4.16 (the "discounted" annuity calculations as in paragraph 4.14), the following position occurs:

	Year 1	Year 5
"the amount charged to revenue" (i.e. the aggregate of depreciation and "interest")	£33,321	£22,744
"sums payable in respect of hire (i.e. rent)	£28,400	£28,400

Which figures should be disclosed? Ideally the accounting basis should be explained and that explanation should mention both the charge to revenue and the sum payable.

4.26 If disclosure is not to be as full as this, the only legal construction that can be put on the phraseology would, in our view, require that the following amounts should be disclosed:-

Year 1	**The sums payable (because the excess, although charged to revenue, must have been charged "in respect of" something other than sums payable)**	£28,400
Year 5	**The amount charged to revenue (because the rest of the sums payable have been charged to something other than revenue)**	£22,744

This demonstrates that a company which discloses only the absolute minimum required by law will almost certainly be disclosing figures which have no meaning, and which certainly cannot be regarded as showing a true and fair view. This reinforces our view that both the charge to revenue and the sum payable should be shown.

EVALUATING THE BENEFITS OF LEASING

4.27 We have commented repeatedly that leasing will often be a more economic method, compared to outright purchase, of obtaining the use of an asset. The usual reasons for this are:-

a) Cash flow: lease rents, being spread over the period of the lease, should prove easier to fund than the full purchase price. Even it if is necessary to borrow to meet some or all of the rental payments, the maximum level of borrowing would be less than in the case of outright purchase.

b) Borrowing limits: leasing as such is not usually treated as a form of borrowing for the purposes of debenture trust deeds, Articles of Association, or other restrictions on the levels of borrowing. It has not in the past normally been reflected in the lessee's balance sheet at all, and in that sense has not been regarded as a borrowing. As already noted, should it be necessary to borrow in order to meet the lease rents, it would be very unusual if the total borrowing were to be as great as for purchase of the asset.

c) Cost: in cases where the lessor can obtain the immediate benefit of tax allowances, and builds this into his quoted rates, a lessee, who could not himself have taken the allowances so promptly, because he has insufficient taxable profits can find that leasing is less costly than purchase, in terms of total outlay.

The same principles apply when lessors are able to reflect in their quoted rates the benefits which they may have been able to obtain in the form of discounts on bulk purchases of the assets concerned, or the availability of finance at advantageous rates.

d) Particular tax benefits of car leasing: lessors can in many cases obtain the 100% first year allowance on cars they lease out, whereas other purchasers could only obtain the 25% writing down allowance (and even this is restricted in the case of cars costing over £5,000). Further, a provision designed to restrict the lessee's right to a deduction for rentals has been found to be generally ineffective—it does not prevent the lessee from getting tax relief on the whole rental paid for a car costing over £5,000. (We will look in paragraphs 5.23–5.26 at the detailed tax rules, and the reasons why they operate in this way).

4.28 It is interesting and instructive to examine a specific transaction to identify and quantify these potential benefits.

Lombard North Central has produced the following table to illustrate what they describe as the "benefit of the lower cash flow from leasing". It shows a benefit, net after tax, of £116 derived from the leasing rather than the purchase of a £3,000 car.

COMPARATIVE CASH FLOW

(Quarters)	1st	2nd	3rd	4th	5th	
Outright purchase	3091	3185	3281	3380	3483	
Leasing	275	559	852	1153	1463	
Net difference	2816	2626	2429	2227	2020	
Interest @ ½% per month on net diff. between outright purchase and leasing	42	39	37	33	30	
Tax relief on interest						
(Quarters)	**6th**	**7th**	**8th**	**9th**	**Subsequent**	**Totals**
Outright purchase	3588	3697	3203	1703	1099	
Leasing	1783	2112	1834	1834	1167	
Net difference	1805	1585	1369	(131)	(68)	
Interest @ ½% per month on net diff. between outright purchase and leasing	27	24	21	(4)	(6)	243
Tax relief on interest			79		48	127
BENEFIT OF THE LOWER CASH FLOW FROM LEASING						116

Interest is assumed to be charged at 1% per month on the outlay incurred on the footing that this outlay would need to be funded from the company's bank borrowing at the beginning of its financial year.

This way of looking at the benefit of leasing is one way of comparing the alternatives. It is vital that we understand just what Lombard North Central are doing, and what they are not even pretending to do. They say that their figures "ignore the adverse net difference between the final cash flow figures". To see just what is the real meaning of their figures, we need to reconstruct their lease figures in full.

4.29 It is not too difficult to deduce the assumptions upon which their cash flow has been calculated. These are

a) The purchase, or commencement of lease, takes place at the beginning of the company's accounting year.

b) The company's tax payment date, is nine months and one day after the end of its accounting period, and it is able to take advantage at that time of the allowances available to it on its purchase of the car, and on interest it had paid.

c) The car will be sold immediately before the end of the second year—its anticipated sale proceeds being £1,500, receivable at the beginning of the third year.

d) Lombard North Central would be prepared to quote a lease rental of £90 per month for a two year term—each month's rental being due at the beginning of the month.

e) The company borrows the whole of the funds needed, whether for purchase or for lease rentals, at a rate of 1% per month, calculated on monthly rests. In fact the interest due (but not paid) has been taken into the Lombard North Central calculations of the amounts of outstanding borrowing up to the end of year 2. That borrowing is treated as if it were interest free in year 3, but this does not cause any significant distortion for our comparison of the two methods, since the total outstandings at the end of year 2 are not wildly different.

What we are not able to determine conclusively is what, if any, participation the lessee may be given in the proceeds of sale. It is true that he has obtained a benefit in the sense that anticipated proceeds of £1,500 have been taken into account in determining the rentals. Sometimes a system operates whereby the lessee could pay a final lease rental, in this case £1,500, and on the sale of the vehicle would receive a rebate of rentals equivalent to (say) 90% of the proceeds. The lessee benefits if proceeds are higher than anticipated, but loses if they are lower. Another possibility is that without a final rental being called for, the rebate of rentals would apply only if and to the extent that proceeds exceeded £1,500. He would then stand to gain, but would be protected from loss. A third possibility is that the lease terms provide for no such participation. On the facts we have, we cannot determine what Lombard North Central is offering.

4.30 The Lombard North Central comparison is as follows:-

			Purchase		Lease
Year 1 Q1	Purchase at beginning of month 1		£3,000		–
	Rent at beginning of months 1, 2 and 3		–		£ 270
	Interest		91		5
			£3,091		£ 275
Q2	Rent at beginning of months 4, 5 and 6		–		270
	Interest		94		14
			£3,185		£ 559
Q3	Rent at beginning of months 7, 8 and 9		–		270
	Interest		96		23
			£3,281		£ 852
Q4	Rent at beginning of months 10, 11 and 12		–		270
	Interest		99		31
			£3,380		£1,153
Year 2 Q1	Rent at beginning of months 1, 2 and 3		103		270
	Interest				40
			£3,483		£1,463
Q2	Rent at beginning of months 4, 5 and 6		–		270
	Interest		105		50
			£3,588		£1,783
Q3	Rent at beginning of months 7, 8 and 9		–		270
	Interest		109		59
			£3,697		£2,112
Q4	Rent at beginning of months 10, 11 and 12		–		270
	Tax relief on year 1 rents		–	1,080 52%	(562)
	Tax relief on year 1 interest	380 52%	(198)	73 52%	(38)
	Capital allowance at 25% of 3,000 =	750 52%	(390)		–
	Interest		94		52
			£3,203		£1,834
Year 3 Q1	Sale proceeds at beginning of year		(1,500)		–
			1,703		1,834
Q2 and Q3			–		–
			1,703		1,834
Q4 T	Tax relief on year 2 rents		–	1,080 52%	(562)
	Tax relief on year 2 interest	411 52%	(214)	201 52%	(105)
	Capital allowance—balancing adjustment	750 52%	(390)		–
			£1,099		£1,167

4.31 The cash flow figures set out in paragraph 4.30 can be summarised in a more assimilable manner as follows:-

		Purchase		Lease
Purchase price of car		£3,000		
Less disposal proceeds		1,500		
		£1,500		
Rents—24 x £90				£2,160
Less tax relief on above at 52%		780		1,124
		£ 720		£1,036
Interest paid in year 1	£ 380		£ 73	
year 2	411		201	
	£ 791		£ 274	
Less tax relief on above at 52%	412	379	143	131
		£1,099		£1,167

The lessee is quite clearly out of pocket to the extent of £68 more than is the purchaser. This amount is the "adverse net difference between the final cash flow figures" which Lombard North Central stated in paragraph 4.28 above they had not taken into account in their presentation of the benefit they were demonstrating.

4.32 Restating these cost figures in the manner in which they will appear in the profit and loss accounts of purchaser and lessee leads to an identical conclusion.

			Purchase		Lease
Year 1	Depreciation	750			
	Rents			1,080	
	Interest	380		73	
		1,130		1,153	
	Less Tax relief	588	542	600	553
Year 2	Depreciation	750			
	Rents			1,080	
	Interest	411		201	
		1,161		1,281	
	Less Tax relief	604	557	667	614
			1,099		1,167

It still costs £68 more to lease than to purchase. This is not an unexpected result. The real advantage of leasing, in profit and loss account terms, arises when the lessee is unable to use the first year allowances, and/or where the lease is entered into close to the lessor's year-end, so that the benefit to him of those allowances is delayed only by the minimum period, (see comment in paragraph 5.06). In practice the volume of leasing business written in the final quarter of the accounting year of most lessors is significantly higher than in other quarters.

4.33 It is also worth noting that when we are using a period as short as two years for the comparison, and also using a straight-line depreciation charge, the profit and loss impact in the first year is more or less identical on either basis.

4.34 It is when we look at the comparative levels of borrowing that we can see a potentially different picture emerging. These borrowings can be illustrated graphically as follows:-

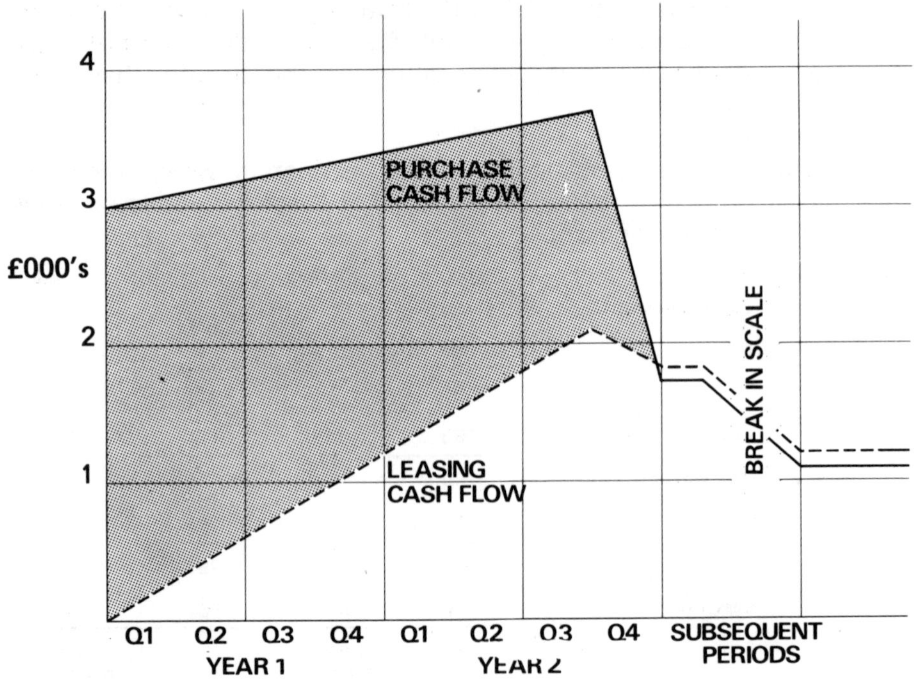

The assumption made by Lombard North Central is that the company would borrow at the maximum level, whether it needed those borrowed funds for the purchase of an asset or not. Further, that funds which had been borrowed, but which were not to be employed for the provision of the asset could be used to generate profits at the rate of 1.5% per month (19.6% per annum).

4.35 The net benefit of £116 worked out by Lombard North Central is therefore the after tax result of applying ½% per month to the shaded area of the graph. The lessee borrows at 1% per month (12.6% per annum) not just the amounts of cash shown on the lower line as his needs for the payment of rentals but the same amount as he would have done had he purchased the asset. The leasing benefit comes from the profitable use of the "spare" funds.

Two points need to be made:-

a) Businesses should be profitable—but additional profits are not the invariable and predictable result of further borrowing.

b) Even assuming that one can anticipate additional net profits of £116 being generated from the additional borrowing, one must still recognise that the lessee starts with a disadvantage of £68 (see paragraphs 4.31 and 4.32). The real comparison throws up a net benefit of £48.

4.36 Explaining the calculation as we have in the last two paragraphs appears to cast some considerable doubt on its validity, but this is to overstate the position:-

a) We must recognise that the "borrowing" position is not the whole of the lessee's or the purchaser's cash flow situation—all that we are looking at is the single element pertaining to the asset. This enters, with all the other elements, into the purchaser/lessee's net cash position.

   If he borrows to purchase the asset he is not necessarily overdrawn at the bank at the end of the third quarter of year 2 by £3,697. But he is, of course, worse off by £3,697 compared to the position he would have been in if he had not purchased the asset, and worse off by £1,585 compared to the position if he had leased the asset.

b) It is this last figure of £1.585 of additional debt (or of reduction in liquidity) which has some significance. If the trader cannot borrow the additional amount because his creditors will not lend it to him, or because his debenture trust deed prevents him, then leasing will be his only course.

In the light of this, Lombard North Central's concept of additional borrowing (being used profitably in the company's trading) is not so far from the mark as it seemed at first. It is also relevant here to think in terms of "marginal rates of return" i.e. what additional amount of profit can be generated by the business which has the use of the asset concerned, compared with the level of its profit without that asset?

4.37 What is also interesting and instructive is to look at Lombard North Central's own position on the basis of the information we have available.

The normal "cash invested in the lease" calculation could be arrived at simply by taking the net difference at each quarter end between the purchase column and the lease column in paragraph 4.30. The purchase of the car would give rise to the same outflows for Lombard North Central, assuming that that company's year end coincided with that of the trader who envisaged purchasing the car, as it would for that company. The leasing of the car to that trader would provide inflows to Lombard North Central of the amounts shown in the column illustrating that lease.

The implication is that Lombard North Central's profit would be a mere £68—but this overlooks the fact that from the lessor's standpoint the lease is a tax based one. Lombard North Central is entitled to a 100% first year allowance on its purchase and gets the benefit of this at the beginning of the fourth quarter of year 2. Subsequently the excess allowances are clawed back, and here the assumptions we have made about the underlying lease figures are most important. We assumed that the sale of the car took place at the end of year two. If that is correct the clawing back of excess allowances would take place at the beginning of the fourth quarter of year 3. On the other hand if the sale were at the beginning of year 3, then the allowances would not be clawed back until twelve months later. Let us leave our original assumptions unchanged and see where that puts Lombard North Central.

The extra allowance is £2,250, and the tax benefit is therefore £1,170. Lombard North Central saves interest for a complete year on this figure. The amount of that interest saving, it is of course compounded, is £157. Net after tax this produces a profit increase of £76. Lombard North Central's total profit on this basis is £144, being the aggregate of £68 and £76. If the clawing back of the allowances were to take place twelve months later, in the fourth quarter of year 4, the profit would be higher by £80, at £224.

4.38 But the basis used in the preceding paragraph for working out Lombard North Central's profit contains two assumptions which are so dubious that our answer must be invalid. Lombard North Central probably would have been able to acquire the car for less than £3,000, because of the quantity of business it does with the supplier. Certainly it would have been able to borrow funds at less than 1% per month (12.6% per annum). We should therefore have applied a lower interest rate in both of the purchase column and the lease column, rather than taking each as they stood in paragraph 4.30.

4.39 This leads us to the really critical question in evaluating the benefits of disadvantages of leasing.

Using funds whose cost was 1% per month (12.6% per annum), it was £48 cheaper over the two year period, for the customer to lease the £3,000 car than to buy it. If the cost of funds had been 1.2% per month (15.4% per annum) this advantage would have disappeared.

Clearly in a short lease, a proportionately larger increase in the borrowing costs would be required in order to change the company's decision. If the lease were for five or ten years, a very small change in the level of interest costs can become critical.

4.40 Deciding whether to lease or buy is seldom any easy decision. The difficulties do not, however, excuse us from making the effort to decide rationally and this means that comparisons must be made by the most rigorous analysis of known facts and anticipated events.

CHAPTER 5 – TAXATION

Contents

INTRODUCTION

5.01 We now turn our attention to taxation, and it may come as no surprise to readers that the picture which emerges in this chapter appears to be lacking in design and coherence. As we have seen in relation to accounting, progress has consisted of a number of ad hoc responses by the accounting profession and others to a strongly expanding leasing industry, responses which have not often been logically consistent. The taxation of leasing arrangements has evolved in a similar way, except that the mechanisms used to create and when necessary to change our tax laws are even less responsive to the needs of taxpayers and of the Inland Revenue.

INTERACTION OF TAX AND ACCOUNTING

5.02 It is worth noting at the outset that there are a number of areas in which the tax outcome and the accounting answers interact with each other in such a way that neither can be dealt with in isolation.

FIRST YEAR ALLOWANCE AND THE INVESTMENT PERIOD METHOD

5.03 The major example of this is the obtaining of first year allowances on an asset whose lease is to be accounted for under the investment period method. If those allowances are obtained, and if the lessor or his group of companies has tax capacity to absorb them, then a substantial tax benefit is receivable nine months after the end of the accounting period in which the lease was written. (The nine months interval is the standard gap between the end of the accounting period and the tax payment date for post—1965 companies. For companies in existence before corporation tax was introduced in 1965, the gap may be longer).

However, if a first year allowance is not received for some reason, then the tax benefit will arise in smaller amounts and the whole shape of the cash flow and the level of the final profit will be materially altered. This will in turn alter both the length of the investment period and the profit to be spread through it.

5.04 The denial of first year allowances may not be known until after the accounts have been prepared and filed with the Inland Revenue. But meanwhile assumptions about the investment period figures have to be made in order to prepare those accounts.

If the lessor cannot demonstrate with a reasonable degree of certainty that the allowances will be given and that the tax benefit from them will materialise, the prudent course is to account without taking credit for that tax benefit unless the lease contains an adjustment clause requiring the lessee to increase his rental payments if the lessor fails to get his first year allowance—the increased rent being designed to preserve the implicit rate of return in the changed circumstances. The problem in this latter case is one of evaluating for the purposes of the accounts whether, and, if so, how soon, the lessee will agree to make the further payments called for.

5.05 If accounts have been prepared on the reasonable assumption that a first year allowance would be received, and it is not, then income will almost certainly have been recognised incorrectly. There is no alternative but to adjust in the next year's accounts.

This may well be a disaster in profit and loss account terms, because a lease which has been written as if it were tax based, (and without an adjustment clause to cover this), may well turn out to be a loss maker without the tax relief. If a loss is anticipated it must of course be fully provided as soon as it becomes apparent that this will be the outcome.

INTERACTION OF TAX AND PRICING

5.06 Tax also interacts with the financial accounts in another, and totally different way. Tax relief arising from a first year allowance will generally be received nine months after the end of the lessor's accounting year. The effect of this relief is considerable, both on the level of investment in the lease, and on the cash flow in general. As a result the lessee can afford to quote more competitive terms at the end of his financial year, when he has less time to wait before receiving his tax benefits, than he could quote at the beginning of the year.

CAPITAL ALLOWANCES FOR TRADING LESSOR

5.07 Turning our attention to the tax legislation we will first of all examine capital allowances. The main base is the 1971 Finance

Act, which substantially rewrote the capital allowance legislation for plant acquired after 27 October 1970. Subsequent Finance Acts have contained a considerable number of amendments, many designed to prevent tax avoidance.

REQUIREMENTS FOR FIRST YEAR ALLOWANCES

5.08 We can only make sense of the legislation if we deal initially with the First Year Allowance (FYA). Under S. 41 FA 1971 where there is:-

a) a trader, who

b) incurs

c) capital expenditure on

d) the provision of

e) machinery or plant

f) for the purposes of the trade

and

g) in consequence of his incurring the expenditure, the machinery or plant belongs to him at some time during the chargeable period related to the incurring of the expenditure,

there is made to him a FYA of 100% for the period related to his incurring of the expenditure. For trading companies the making of an allowance is in the Revenue's view mandatory under S. 73 CAA 1968, and therefore provision is specifically made in S. 41(3) FA 1971 to enable the company to disclaim the FYA, or to take a percentage lower than the full 100%.

5.09 It is perhaps advisable to consider briefly the seven requisites, (a) to (g) set out in the preceding paragraph. A company whose trade is, or includes, the leasing of machinery or plant to customers is undoubtedly regarded as furnishing those assets for the purposes of its trade when it lets them. The same would hold true of assets acquired by the company with a view to their being leased to customers in the course of the trading operations, but which were not let before the end of the accounting period in which they were acquired.

5.10 The word "provision" of machinery or plant is generally taken to be wider than the word acquisition. Providing the assets must include not only purchasing them, or constructing them, but also transporting and, if necessary, adapting them so as to be able to let them.

5.11 Expenditure is incurred when it becomes payable, (S. 50(4) FA 1971). Where a company has not commenced trading at the time it actually incurs its expenditure on providing machinery or plant, it is deemed to have incurred the expenditure on the first day of trading. In this way, the FYA is not denied, because the date of deemed-incurring falls within and not outside an accounting period related to that trade for corporation tax purposes (S. 50(4) FA 1971).

PAYMENTS ON ACCOUNT

5.12 The legislation somewhat curiously does not refer to payments on account. To take the example of the building of a ship, the contract will normally stipulate a series of payments on account during the construction phase, a further payment after launch to cover the fitting of engines, and then a final payment when the ship is handed over to the purchaser after successful trials.

The payer can invoke S.45(1)(a) FA 1971 which enables him to claim allowances as if the plant belonged to him when he incurred the expenditure, i.e., when the payments on account became payable. In fact what was being paid for manifestly would not belong to him until it was handed over to him in a completed state. This does not answer the question whether an incomplete ship is plant at all. (It is not technically a ship until it has had its engines fitted, because the definition of a ship in the Merchant Shipping Act 1879 requires that it be self propelled). But is it plant? S. 50(6) FA 1971 says that plant includes a part of plant, but this is different from saying that it includes something which is not yet plant but may become plant.

The Inland Revenue have indicated that they will not take this point against a taxpayer in any case where the pattern of payments on account is a normal commercial arrangement negotiated at arms length between unconnected parties. Payments on account can therefore be regarded as fulfilling, at the time they are made, all the requirements set out in paragraph 5.08 above.

THE ASSET ALREADY OWNED BEFORE THE EXPENDITURE IS INCURRED

5.13 As a result of the Romalpa case on reservation of title, we could have the following situation, again using the ship building illustration. If the yard has acquired steel, title to which has been reserved by the supplier, and the yard has not paid the supplier, that supplier is entitled to take back his steel. This could be embarrassing for the yard if at the time of seizure the steel concerned was incorporated in an almost completed ship. The building contract between the yard and the customer will frequently try to prevent this possibility by stipulating that as soon as steel is appropriated by the yard to the ship under construction, ownership of that steel passes to the customer. The payments by that customer, on account and finally, remain unaltered. However, it is no longer possible to say that "in consequence of" his incurring the expenditure the constituent steel in the ship belongs to him. It belonged to him already, before the expenditure was incurred. This situation might appear to conflict with S. 41 FA 1971 (see paragraph 5.08) and therefore fall outside the requirements set out.

The Revenue have confirmed that they will turn a blind eye to this technicality.

DEFINITION OF CAPITAL EXPENDITURE

5.14 There is no explicit definition in the tax legislation of the phrase "capital expenditure". All that the statutes tell us is that if payments are classified as annual payments, then they are not capital expenditure. It is generally necessary to look at the tax position of the recipient in order to determine whether a payment to him is an annual payment for the payer, because this is one of the few cases in which the treatment in payer's hands and in the recipient's must mirror each other. The Inland Revenue are however very clear in their minds what "capital expenditure" means. The concept is the pure economic meaning of fixed capital as originally defined by Adam Smith: "Fixed capital is what the owner turns to profit by keeping it in his own possession, and circulating capital is what he makes profit of by parting with it and letting it change masters". Capital allowances are a form of tax relief to be made available only to the taxpayer who keeps his plant in his own possession. (Perhaps Adam Smith would have said ownership rather than possession if he had foreseen leasing).

The taxpayer who intends, or can be suspected of intending, to dispose of his plant in order to realise a profit is not holding it as fixed capital. The expenditure he incurred was not capital expenditure. His tax relief for what we might now call stock in trade comes in a very different series of forms, for instance the ability to restate the asset at the lower of cost or net realisable value, and to deduct the diminution.

This distinction accounts for the fact that capital allowances usually go to the lessor in leasing and to the purchaser in a hire purchase transaction. We will now examine four particular aspects where problems occur.

5.15 First those lessors who manufacture the product which they subsequently lease to their customers will only be regarded as having incurred expenditure up to the level of their actual costs.

We have suggested in paragraph 3.03 that a manufacturer-lessor who disposes of his product through a full pay-out lease can and should recognise a manufacturing profit separate from his leasing profit—that he should in other words transfer the product to his leasing operation at a figure which includes cost and manufacturing profit.

That may be acceptable for accounting purposes, but not for tax—unless the manufacturer and the lessor are separate corporate entities.

5.16 Secondly the capital expenditure on the provision of machinery or plant does not include the costs of finance. Thus, the trading company which borrows money for the provision of machinery to its customers does not thereby increase the capital allowance "cost" of the machinery by the amount of interest payable on those borrowings. This interest will normally qualify either as a trading expense or as a charge on income—it is not and cannot be claimed to be a part of the capital cost of the machinery.

The same principle also holds true for those "one-off" financial costs sometimes met when borrowings are arranged. The commission paid to the lender for his undertaking a "commitment" to lend is one example. Another is the insurance premium which he may insist the borrower pays—insuring the lender against bad debts.

5.17 Thirdly, the Inland Revenue's view of currency differences is that they form no part of the capital expenditure on provision of machinery or plant. The expenditure qualifying for allowances is quantified in sterling at the rate of exchange ruling at the "incurred" date. If early or late payment through the exchanges results in a higher sterling cost, then the difference is not a part of the capital cost of providing the machinery or plant.

This is of course the complete opposite to the position obtaining in trading transactions e.g. where U.S. dollars are acquired as the first, (and integral), part of a commercial transaction consisting of purchasing tobacco leaf, the costs deductible as relating to that leaf would include currency differences as well as the translated purchase price. (Imperial Tobacco Co. v Kelly—25 TC 292).

5.18 The fourth aspect over which care needs to be taken when interpreting the phrase "capital expenditure on the provision of machinery or plant" is as follows. Lessor companies frequently find that for commercial or tax reasons applying particularly to them at a given moment, it is advisable for them to enlarge or to contract their "book". Lessor A wishing to take on more business may agree to purchase from Lessor B a number of the latter's current leases, at a point when Lessor B would be better suited with a lump sum than by the flow of income that those leases would produce if retained.

5.19 The legal ownership of the leased assets undoubtedly passes from B to A, and the sum which A pays is undoubtedly capital. But it could be that at least some part of the capital sum could be attributed to the purchase by A not of machinery, but of contracts assuring him a flow of future income. Consider, for instance, a block of business consisting solely of five year, full pay-out, leases of motor cars—each lease being one year old, and having four years to run. It is more or less certain that the market value of the cars themselves would be less than the value of the leases. We have no information how keen a purchaser A is, or to what extent B is under pressure to sell, but it is at least possible that A could be said to be paying over the odds if all that he was buying was year-old second hand cars. To the extent that he does over-pay, the excess is an outflow which does not fit into any of the categories of expenditure which qualify for tax relief.

In practice the Inland Revenue do not appear to take this point against established leasing companies, but it is a point that should be watched.

5.20 The specific areas of difficulty looked at in paragraphs 5.15 to 5.19 have been the quantifying of the capital expenditure of manufacturer lessors, the finance costs of the currency fluctuation differences, and the purchase of portfolios rather than the purchase of plant.

The fundamental point, however, which is far more important than any of these is the Adam Smith concept set out in paragraph 5.14. It would not perhaps be overstating the position if we were to describe lessors as balanced on a knife edge. There is a House of Lords decision dating from just after the first world war, (Gloucester Wagon Co. 12 TC 720), which is still regarded by the Revenue as binding. The company in that case had a trade of renting out railway wagons. From time to time, when the wagons concerned became too worn and old to rent, the company sold them off. At that time, sales which were "capital" were outside the scope of tax altogether, so that these sales of surplus wagons did not give rise to taxable income for the company. However, shortly after the first war, the company decided to sell the whole of its stock of wagons. The House of Lords unanimously held that what the company was doing in this instance was turning to profitable (trading) account its trading stocks—that it was not the same transaction as the sale of fixed assets which had come to the end of their (capital) life.

The sting in the tail of this case is this. Consider a company which has a trade that includes selling certain types of plant outright whether it manufactures them or buys them in, and also, as a part of that same trade, it leases out that same type of plant. On the Gloucester Wagon basis, this whole activity has been held to be a single trading operation. There is no clear distinction between the item of plant which is held for sale, and the identical item which is held for lease. The expenditure incurred on manufacturing or purchasing the latter is not capital expenditure. The leasing transactions should certainly be handled in a separate company from the outright sales, but this is far from being a complete and totally safe solution. The knife edge is still there. We ignore it at our peril.

WITHDRAWAL OF FIRST YEAR ALLOWANCES

5.21 First year allowances may be withdrawn or withheld in the same circumstances from a company trading as a lessor as from any other trader:-

a) Where the chargeable period in which the expenditure is incurred is also that in which the trade is permanently discontinued (S. 41(1) FA 1971);

b) Where the machinery or plant ceases to belong to the trader without having been brought into use for the purposes of his trade (S. 41(2) FA 1971);

c) In the cases of purchases within the anti-avoidance provisions in Sch 8(3)(1) FA 1971, that is to say those where vendor and purchaser are connected, those where the machinery or plant continues to be used by the vendor or a person connected with him, and those where the sole or main benefit appears to be the obtaining of capital allowances;

d) Where the machinery or plant is used for purposes of business entertainment or is used partly for purposes unconnected with the trade. We believe that in the case of leased plant the following is the correct analysis. The lessor is "using" the plant in his trade of leasing, and should therefore suffer no loss of allowances. If the lessee then uses the item for business entertaining, or for non-business purposes, it is he who should suffer some disallowance of the expenditure which he has incurred, i.e. of the rentals he pays.

5.22 There are also a number of other anti-avoidance provisions in the legislation since 1971, to which we shall return in paragraphs 5.95 et seq below.

FIRST YEAR ALLOWANCES ON PRIVATE CARS

5.23 A first year allowance is given to a trading lessor in respect of cars leased to his customers. This is regarded by some as an anomaly as it would not be available to those customers if they themselves had purchased the cars concerned.

This results from the definition in S. 43 FA 1971 of those classes of vehicles for which first year allowances are not granted. Instead of defining specifically the private cars to be excluded, the legislation first excludes all vehicles and then excludes from that exclusion three defined categories. The first two of these are vehicles primarily suited for the conveyance of goods and those not of a type commonly used as private vehicles and which are unsuited for such use. The third category excluded comprises vehicles provided wholly or mainly for hire in the course of a trade to members of the public. A company whose trade is the leasing of cars, just as much as the operator of a fleet of coaches, is therefore entitled to first year allowances.

5.24 The Revenue admit that finance lessors are just as much involved in letting cars to the public in the course of their trade as are the self-drive hire companies. They therefore accept that the lessor is entitled to a first year allowance.

The acceptance follows a decision in 1975 of the Special Commissioners of Income Tax that first year allowances are available to the owner of cars "let on contract hire to a particular customer or let on fleet hire to other companies".

5.25 The Revenue do make a qualification to this in that first year allowances are given only to those who are "genuinely in business as car hirers". They interpret this as meaning that the lessor must be prepared to deal with any prospective customer, (subject to commercial considerations about his suitability) and that the letting is a genuine commercial venture vis-a-vis the public.

The letting of cars to "the public" does not cover letting only to a limited range of customers, for instance letting only to business connections or associates. It specifically does not embrace the group company whose activity is the letting of cars only to other companies in its own group.

PRIVATE CARS–DEDUCTION OF RENT CHARGES

5.26 The anomaly, if such it be, in the definition of private cars does not end there.

Sch 8 FA 1971, contains in paragraphs 10, 11 and 12 certain restrictions relating to cars costing more than £5,000. In the first two of those paragraphs, writing down allowances are limited to £1,250 per annum until such time as the written down value of the vehicle falls below £5,000; from then on the allowance is calculated in the normal way at 25%.

The third of the three paragraphs requires that a disallowance, (not just a deferment of relief), be made where a car costing more than £5,000 is hired. The disallowance is that proportion of the annual rental which is represented by the excess of the car's cost over £5,000 as a fraction of that cost. "Motor car" for the purposes of all three of these paragraphs is defined in paragraph 9 of the schedule and once again specifically excludes vehicles provided wholly or mainly for hire to members of the public.

Members of that public who intend to use leased cars for their own business purposes can therefore hire them from a leasing company.

a) in the knowledge that the lessor will be entitled to first year allowances, and

b) knowing that the rental charge will be deductible in full by the lessee despite the apparent intent in paragraph 12.

5.27 The word "anomaly" is almost certainly a misconception. In tax law the words generally do mean what they say. Moreover what they say and what they mean is what our legislators meant them to say and to mean. Anomalies more often than not are the deliberate choices of those who framed our tax laws.

FIRST YEAR ALLOWANCE PERCENTAGES

5.28 First year allowances are currently 100%, unless disclaimed or taken at a reduced percentage. A considerable amount, if not the whole of a trading lessor's expenditure, will qualify for these allowances. It may therefore seem somewhat superfluous to go on to talk about the writing down allowances available on the remainder of the expenditure.

WRITING DOWN ALLOWANCES AND BALANCING ADJUSTMENTS

5.29 This is to misunderstand the reality. Writing down allowances may not be a large part of the total allowances available. Balancing adjustments can however be highly significant. Both require calculation, and the calculation of both is, as we shall see, part of a single operation. The main legislative provision is S. 44 FA 1971.

QUALIFYING EXPENDITURE FOR WRITING DOWN ALLOWANCES

5.30 We are directed first to identify and quantify the trader's qualifying expenditure.

Expenditure only falls into this category if the plant on which it was incurred is, or has been, in use for trading purposes. (First year allowances are not dependant upon the item having been used; it is sufficient that the plant was acquired for the purposes of the trade. FYA are only withdrawn under S. 41(2) FA 1971 if the plant ceases to belong to the trader without having previously been used).

5.31 Expenditure is qualifying expenditure only if it fits into one or other of the following four categories:-

a) Expenditure in the period which could not qualify for a FYA. (A disclaimer of FYA does not bring the expenditure into this category).

b) The preceding period's expenditure to the extent that there is any residue of it left after deduction of that period's FYA's.

c) Any amount remaining, after deducting the preceding period's disposal values and writing down allowances, of that period's qualifying expenditure (that is to say the equivalent amounts brought into that year's calculations from its equivalent of (a) (b) and this subparagraph);

d) Expenditure on plant, less its disposal value, where that plant ceases to belong to the trader without his ever having brought it into use (Sch 8(4) FA 1971).

ABORTIVE EXPENDITURE

5.32 At one time the Revenue used to maintain strongly that capital allowances could not be granted on expenditure which proved abortive, in that what resulted from it could not be described as plant. The final result of the expenditure could be, for instance, merely a study of the design possibilites, and of the material availability, for a proposed new machine.

If that Revenue view was ever right, it must in the author's view be now discredited. It was held to be wrong in the case of CIR v George Guthrie and Son (33TC 327). In that case the taxpayer spent £1,400 on the provision of a van. He never got his van, because the vendor fraudulently made off with the money. In the Court of Session, Lord Cooper said:
"When, as in this case, there has been a bona fide expenditure of capital for an approved purpose, I consider that the Special Commissioners were justified in concluding that their concern was with the fact and the object of the expenditure and not with the subsidiary question whether the money was well spent or ill spent, or whether (bona fides being always assumed) the intended object was or was not actually realised".

The Revenue's response was to enact the provision already examined in paragraph 5.08(g), requiring that in consequence of the taxpayer's incurring the expenditure, the plant and machinery must "belong" to him. The van never did.

However, in our view what is important in relation to the case quoted above is not the Revenue's attempt to negate it by amendment of the law, but the breadth of the wording used by the Court of Session. Lord Reid in the later Barclay Curle Drydock case (45 TC 239) referred to the Guthrie case and went on to say expenditure on the "provision of" plant was wider than that on plant itself; that if expenditure must be incurred before the plant can be provided, one is misdirecting oneself if one says that it is too remote. It seems clear that in cases where some preliminary works or studies must be carried out before the tangible "plant" is installed and operating, these works and studies are "plant". Even if they are abortive, and no tangible item results, they still qualify.

In any event, the case of McVeigh v Arthur Sanderson and Sons (45 TC 273) in the High Court in 1968 proved unequivocally that wallpaper manufacturers were entitled to allowances on the cost of designs they did not use as well as those which they did.

DISPOSAL VALUES

5.33 We have noted in paragraph 5.31 the requirement that disposal values have to be deducted from the amounts of the qualifying expenditure. We therefore need to be able to recognise a disposal value when we see one. S. 44(6) FA 1971 outlines five separate events which give rise to a disposal value:-

a) sale of the plant, other than a sale within (b) below.

b) sale at less than full value, except for those cases where the buyer is entitled to claim capital allowances on his acquisition cost.

c) demolition or destruction of the plant.

d) permanent loss of the plant.

e) cessation of the trade.

The section then provides a catch-all, (f), described as "any other event" which necessitates a balancing adjustment. Since the two broad categories of necessitating events in S. 44(5) are those by which the plant ceases to belong to the trader, and those by which it ceases to be used in his trade, it is clear that a permanent taking out of use would be within the catch-all. The disposal value for plant in (b) and (f) is its open market value. That for plant in (a), (c) and (d) can be regarded as the net proceeds received by the trader. And where (e) precedes an (a), (b), (c) or (d) event, then one looks at that subsequent happening to find a disposal value. In every case disposal value includes insurance proceeds and other compensation so far as these consist of capital sums. In no case can disposal value exceed original cost.

DEMOLITION COSTS

5.34 Until recently no allowance could be obtained for demolition costs, these being regarded as capital, but not falling within the capital allowance requirements. Now demolition costs, net of any sale proceeds of the demolished item, are to be added to the cost of its replacement. If the item is not replaced, they may be added to qualifying expenditure.

CALCULATION OF ALLOWANCES

5.35 The structure of the writing down allowance/balancing adjustment legislation S. 44 FA 1971) is that

a) The qualifying expenditure for the period is calculated as in paragraph 5.31 above.

b) The disposal values of all plant which has ceased to belong to the trader in the period, or has ceased to be used, are calculated as in paragraph 5.33 above.

If (b) exceeds (a), then the trader is taxable on the excess, that tax being charged by treating the excess as if it were a trading receipt (S. 73(2) CAA 1968).

If (a) exceeds (b), then the trader receives an allowance of 25% of the excess—unless the period is that in which he ceases trading, in which case he receives an allowance of 100%.

5.36 It is appropriate at this point to draw attention to two points which result from the way in which the writing down allowance and balancing adjustment section is designed to operate. In our experience, neither is widely understood. These two points concern:-

a) Whether there is necessarily always a disadvantage in a company's being unable to claim a first year allowance.

b) Lessee participation in disposal proceeds.

IS IT ALWAYS DISADVANTAGEOUS NOT TO QUALIFY FOR A FIRST YEAR ALLOWANCE?

5.37 A first year allowance cannot be claimed in respect of plant purchased from a connected company, Sch 8(3)(1)(a) FA 1971.

If, in the year in which the trader acquires plant in this way, his qualifying expenditure looks like this:-

a)	Expenditure in the period not qualifying for FYA (purchase from connected company)	£800
b)	Expenditure of preceding period after deducting FYA of that period	Nil
c)	Balance of qualifying expenditure brought forward from preceding period	£200
	Total	£1,000

but, in that same year, the trader also has disposal values equal to or in excess of £1,000, then the non availability of first year allowances does not matter because he achieves the same tax position as if he had been able to claim them.

It is however important to note that this applies only where the trader could not take FYA's. If he was technically entitled to them, but did in fact disclaim, then the relevant expenditure would not fall into (a) above. It would fall into the next year's category (b). As a condition of granting exchange control permission for some purchases of equipment from abroad, the Bank of England sometimes exacts an undertaking from the trader that he will disclaim his FYA.

LESSEE PARTICIPATION IN DISPOSAL PROCEEDS

5.38 The second point, which is sometimes misunderstood, relates to leases in which the lessee participates in the proceeds when the asset is sold after the end of the lease term.

There are two ways in which his participation can be drafted in the lease. In the more common phraseology, the lessee is allowed a monetary amount equal to x% of the sale proceeds, "by way of rebate of hire". It is normal to recognise that a "rebate of hire" cannot exceed the hire previously paid. The clause will therefore limit the amount the lessee can receive to the aggregate of his payments. This quite clearly puts the sum into the lessee's trading receipts, and into the lessor's deductible expenses, both in the year in which the amount is payable.

On the other hand it is possible for the lease to grant the lessee x% of the proceeds, directly. In our view the lessor cannot then claim that he is entitled to deduct the amount concerned in calculating trading profits; but he is absolutely entitled to say that the disposal value to be brought in should only be (100 - x)%. This accords precisely with the wording of S. 44(6)(a) FA 1971 requiring him where there has been an open market sale to bring in "the net proceeds to the person in question of the sale". The fact that the vendor does not receive the whole proceeds of sale does not mean that the sale itself was at a lower than open market price, nor does it mean that the vendor must bring in more than his own net proceeds.

5.39 The lessee would still be taxable on his share of the proceeds, although it is debatable whether this would necessarily be a part of his normal trade. It might be a separate "adventure in the nature of trade", this participation in the sale of someone else's assets, and be taxable under Case 1 but separately. Alternatively, it could be a Case VI receipt, as a profit not falling into the trading, or any other, case.

5.40 We have been examining in paragraphs 5.07 to 5.40 the capital allowances normally available to a trading lessor. There are a number of restrictions at which we will look below in paragraphs 5.95 to 5.114 under the general heading of anti-avoidance. (For lessors who are not in the trade of leasing, but whose activities are only peripheral, there are further restrictions on the allowances available, and on the way in which those allowances can be used against income. This is the subject of paragraphs 5.65 et seq below).

LESSOR'S TAX COMPUTATION

5.41 It is now time to turn to the other items in the trading lessor's corporation tax computation.

BAD DEBTS

5.42 The most straightforward of these can be dealt with without difficulty. The amounts charged to profit and loss account as a general provision for doubtful debts are not deductible for tax purposes. Throughout our accounting examples, we have illustrated a provision at 1% of the figure at which the leased asset stands. This must be disallowed.

Deductions can however be claimed for

a) Specific provisions made against particular debts whose collectibility is in question, where the amounts provided are related to the anticipated outturn of the particular transaction.

b) Bad debts incurred to the extent that they exceed specific provisions made under (a) above.

BORROWING COSTS—INTEREST

5.43 The relief for costs of funds borrowed by a lessor is not straightforward. We are of course concerned here with the lessor's borrowings from external sources—the liabilities which appear in his balance sheet—and not with those which are purely notional "investment" by one lease in another.

5.44 Interest can be either a trading expense or a charge on income. If it is the latter, relief is given only on payment, (S. 248(1) TA 1970), whereas interest regarded as an expense would qualify for relief at the point it could properly be provided in the accounts, whether paid or not.

5.45 The prime relief for interest is by way of trading expense. S. 130 (f) TA 1970 specifically says that it is not to be read "as disallowing the deduction of any interest". One moves next to S. 251 TA 1970 which

a) specifically envisages the deduction as a trading expense of annual interest payable to a UK bank;

b) specifically prevents such a deduction for other annual interest;

S. 251 does not specifically allow or disallow a deduction for short interest. This category of interest is therefore not prevented from being deducted by either the general provisions of S. 130 or the specific provisions of S. 251. The result of this absence of any direction to the contrary is that all short interest can be deducted, so long as it meets the overall requirement that it was incurred wholly and exclusively for the purposes of the trade.

What we do need to identify is the difference between annual interest and short interest. Annual interest is interest on a borrowing for a period which could exceed a year, whether or not it does in fact exceed a year. All other interest is short interest.

5.46 To recapitulate at this point, we find ourselves claiming a deduction, as a trading expense, for:-

a) all short interest, because if it cannot be deducted, no other form of tax relief is available for it, except for one very small unlikely eventuality, which can for all practical purposes be ignored;

b) bank interest which is annual interest.

All other interest is treated as a charge on income.

In our experience there is a considerable degree of confusion in the minds of many taxpayers about the foregoing. There is also some lack of comprehension about the significance of a company's being entitled to a deduction as opposed to being entitled to relief for a charge on income. One of the matters which makes it important to know which relief is available has already been mentioned in paragraph 5.44—deductions are given on the basis of amounts accrued in the accounts whether paid or not, whilst charges on income have to be paid in order to qualify for relief. Apart from that there are two other main reasons why the distinction is vital, although probably neither applies in the normal case to lessors. Excess charges on income are treated differently from normal trading losses, which is what excess deductible interest would be, the restrictions being set out in S. 177(8) TA 1970. Secondly, it is necessary for certain purposes to arrive at the amount of trading profits, after deductions but before charges on income. An example is the requirement in Sch 5(9)(2) FA 1976 that 15% of trading profits defined in this way be deducted in arriving at the amount of stock appreciation relief. No company should voluntarily deduct 15% of too high a figure.

We mentioned that our experience has been some degree of confusion over this whole subject. Lest we ourselves create any further confusion, we should perhaps make it clear that the procedure set out above applies to trading companies, but others to which S. 130 (f) and S. 251(3) do not apply, are subject to a different set of rules.

5.47 Relief for interest is only available if that interest is charged against profits in the company's accounts. S. 248(5) TA1970 specifically prevents interest which has been capitalised from qualifying as a charge on income, and any taxpayer who tried to claim a deduction as a trading expense for interest (or any other category of expense) without treating it in his accounts as an expense would be asking for the Revenue to object.

There are however borrowings which are of a capital nature, and borrowings which are trading ones. Relief is available for the interest on either type of borrowing. If the interest is of a kind which can be deducted, then the wording of S. 130(f) TA 1970 is relevant; that section says that the deduction of "any" interest is not prevented. There is no doubt that under this wording the Revenue permit taxpayers to deduct interest on capital borrowings as well as that on borrowings for trading purposes. The provisions giving relief for charges on income contain no prohibition on treating as a charge interest on both types of borrowing.

BORROWING COSTS—EXCHANGE DIFFERENCES

5.48 The difference between capital borrowings and others is, however, vital from the point of view of establishing a deduction for exchange losses. Such losses occurring on the principal sums borrowed are allowed if the borrowings are regarded as being of a "circulating capital" nature, but not if they are of a "fixed capital" nature.

5.49 A bank says that its trade is the taking of deposits and the making of loans. Interest income on the latter and interest expense on the former are integral to its trading results, and deductions are similarly available for bad debts among the loans and for exchange losses on both loans and deposits.

A lessor engaged in writing finance leases also makes its money from a financial transaction—it looks on the source of its profit as being its use of money, and the shape of the flows of incomings and outgoings. Admittedly, the purchase of assets is also a part of the operation, and admittedly also the lessor's expenditure on this needs to be described as "capital" if it is to obtain the capital allowances set out in paragraphs 5.07 et seq.

But, in our view, the use of borrowed funds to finance capital expenditure does not prove, on its own, that the borrowings are fixed capital. The whole shape of the activity needs to be seen in a wider perspective and this may show that many if not all of a lessor's borrowings do circulate.

5.50 If the borrowing itself is integral to the trade, then the act of making it is indisputably a trading operation. From this it follows that any costs, such as exchange losses, associated with the act of borrowing, even if "one off", are nevertheless deductible. The general prohibition on deducting the costs of raising finance, such items as commitment commissions to banks or underwriting expenses in public issues, is based upon these being "capital" expense, because the borrowing is "capital". If the borrowing is not "capital", neither are the costs.

However, each lessor must look at his own situation, and must see each of his borrowings in that context. There can be no general rule applicable to all cases.

TAXABLE INCOME

5.51 Having looked in some depth at the amounts to be taken out of taxable income of a trading lessor. It is necessary that we give some thought to the shape of that income itself.

5.52 A lessor holds fixed assets from which he derives income by holding them, not by parting with them. This is a paraphrase of Adam Smith's distinction between fixed and circulating capital — a distinction which is sometimes extremely difficult to draw in the complexity of modern business operations. It is however clear enough in the case of a lessor for us to be able to see that

a) The assets concerned are fixed assets not stock-in-trade. Reductions in their value are recognised in the tax legislation by way of relief for the capital expenditure incurred on them, not by any possibility that the lessor can restate them at net realisable value if this is less than cost.

b) A gain over original cost is taxable under the capital gains tax rules;

c) Stock Relief is specifically not available under Sch 5(29)(2) (c) 1976 on assets on hire.

TIMING OF TAXABILITY OF RENTS

5.53 The lessor brings in rents as they become due. This is the "accruals" basis of computing income which is normally a requirement of the Inland Revenue. It is unlikely that any leasing company starting business today would be permitted to account for its rents on a cash basis rather than by accruing them.

It is always open to any taxpayer to seek from the Revenue a "conventional" basis of assessment—that is to say a basis under which its income is brought in on a footing other than on accrual. If such a basis is to be agreed, it is necessary for the taxpayer to show that the results will not be very different from those that would be produced by the accruals basis, and that they will remain substantially similar throughout the time the conventional basis continues in use. Even then, the Revenue usually require to have it demonstrated that there is some good reason why the normal arrangements should not or cannot be used.

As we have already briefly noted in paragraph 2.63, bringing in rents on an accruals basis produces for the lessor the same quantum of profit whatever accounting method he uses. This follows from the fact that every accounting method fixes the profit recognition through a variation in the level of the depreciation charge. That depreciation is added back for tax purposes, and capital allowances granted in substitution. The taxable profit is thus unalterable.

5.54 Let us prove this point. In paragraph 3.102, we illustrated a method of accounting for a balloon rental. The lease called for no rent during the first four years, and then required four quarterly payments of £47,630 in the final year.

We showed by illustration how it would be possible to avoid having to provide "negative depreciation" if credit were taken evenly through the lease period for the rents, even though these were not then due:

	Year 1	Year 2	Year 3	Year 4	Year 5	Total
Rent	£ 38,104	£ 38,104	£ 38,104	£ 38,104	£ 38,104	£190,520
Depreciation	(21,821)	(19,420)	(16,663)	(13,500)	(28,596)	(100,000)
	16,283	18,684	21,441	24,604	9,508	90,520
Interest	(14,750)	(16,926)	(19,422)	(22,287)	(8,398)	(81,783)
	1,533	1,758	2,019	2,317	1,110	8,737
Doubtful debts	(1,162)	(188)	(214)	(246)	1,810	–
	£ 371	£ 1,570	£ 1,805	£ 2,071	£ 2,920	£ 8,737
Balance Sheet at end of year						
Asset Amount	78,179	58,759	42,096	28,596	–	
Debtor	38,104	76,208	114,312	152,416	–	
	£116,283	£134,967	£156,408	£181,012	–	

Does this method result in the company being taxed by the end of year 4 on £152,416 of rents which it has not at that stage received, and which it is not due to receive until year 5?

5.55 The answer is no. Lord Reid's statement in the BSC Footwear case has already been quoted in paragraph 2.23, namely that normal principles of commercial accountancy should be used to arrive at taxable profits. The accounts set out in the preceding paragraph have already been described as cosmetic. If the Inland Revenue need accounts on the basis of Lord Reid's statement they will get the accounts set out in paragraph 3.100, that is accounts showing no rent until the final year. But the gross income line in the profit and loss account is exactly the same in both cases; it was, and is, derived directly from the investment period method, a method which we have recognised as eminently commercial. In addition the aggregate of the asset amounts in the balance sheet is also what it was before, although its split between fixed asset and debtor appears different.

Basically, under the powder and paint, nothing has altered. The Inland Revenue can be expected to agree that tax should not change either.

TIMING OF TAXABILITY OF OTHER INCOME

5.56 The accounting method used will affect taxable income in any case where there is income other than the gross income line, rent less depreciation, on which we have been concentrating so heavily. For instance, there is no reason why leasing companies should not have some income of the same type as is normally received by companies in the hire purchase and related financial fields. A substantial part of the total income of such companies takes the form of "fixed finance charges". An asset sold, or a personal loan made, results for the finance company in a flow of cash receipts, each of which represents part payment for the asset and part profit, or part repayment and part interest on the loan. Because neither the asset nor the loan is a "capital" item for the finance company, income recognition operates rather differently. The amounts to be credited against the customer's debt, when each instalment is received, and the balance to be credited to profit, are not determined merely by a chosen level of depreciation charge, as is the case with a leasing company, where the asset is capital. Hire purchase companies usually decide how much is debt repayment, and how much income, using a method exactly similar to the rule of 78 used by lessors.

5,57 The tax computation does not contain any disallowance equivalent to the disallowance of depreciation for lessors, and taxable profits are therefore based much more closely on the income the hire purchase company recognises.

To the extent therefore that leasing companies receive non-rental income of a similar nature to that described above, the accounting methods used will affect their taxable income.

TAXATION OF AMOUNTS RECEIVED UNDER CURRENCY ADJUSTMENT CLAUSES

5.58 This leads us to another major area of doubt and difficulty, namely the taxation of amounts received under adjustment clauses. This can best be illustrated by referring to the problems of currency exposure mentioned in paragraphs 3.38 to 3.41.

In those paragraphs we showed the operation of a currency adjustment clause under which the lessee was liable to pay to the lessor, as additional rent, the following amounts.

a)	The difference between the lessor's sterling cost of paying interest of \$24,356 at \$1.80 = £1	£13,531
	and what it would have cost in sterling had the rate remained \$2.00	12,178
		£ 1,353
b)	The difference between the lessor's sterling cost of repaying dollar borrowing of \$32,444 at \$1.80 = £1	£18,024
	and what it would have cost in sterling had the rate remained \$2.00	16,222
		£ 1,802

5.59 The first of these receipts gives rise to no particular tax difficulty. If exchange rates had remained steady, the lessor would have had tax relief (as a charge on income or as a deduction) for £12,178, this being the sterling equivalent at the time of payment of \$24,356 on the assumption of an unchanged \$2 = £1 exchange rate.

What the lessor does in fact reflect in his tax compuation is the following:-

Tax relief (charge or deduction) being \$24,356 at \$1.80	£13,531
Less additional Case 1 income	1,353
	£12,178

5.60 But when we come to the second item, the tax treatment becomes less clear. If it is to be treated as an addition to the rental receivable by the lessor, it will undoubtedly be taxable. On the other hand, the question whether tax relief can be obtained for the additional cost of repaying the borrowing, so as to offset this additional income, is one which we examined in paragraphs 5.48 to 5.50 without being able to give any conclusive answer. From the lessee's point of view, the additional rent he pays under the currency adjustment clause will be tax deductible.

In order to leave the lessor with the correct amount of cash so that he can meet the additional costs of repaying the loan there are three courses open to lessor and lessee:-

a) Pay the adjustment at an engrossed amount;-

b) Pay the adjustment net, on the assumption that the lessor will get tax relief for those additional costs of repayment;

c) Describe the adjustment as a capital payment.

These three courses are now examined.

5.61 If the first course is followed, and the currency adjustment is paid at an engrossed amount of £3,754, the net cost to the lessee is £1,802.

The lessor receives, and is taxed on, the additional engrossed income. He is again left with £1,802 net. But he will also claim, and may be allowed, tax relief on his loss on the borrowing, this also being a figure of £1,802. If he succeeds, he has obtained a subsidy from the Chancellor of the Exchequer of £1,802 at 52% £937.

So far as the Chancellor is concerned the tax relief of £1,952 (the tax engrossment of £1,802 net) given to the lessee, (assuming, of course, that the lessee has taxable income at 52% to absorb the additional expense), is matched by additional tax of the same amount collected from the lessor.

5.62 The second course is to pay the currency adjustment net. The lessor receives £1,802, and is taxable on this amount. Assuming that he obtains his deduction for the equivalent loss on the repayment of the borrowing, however, he will have achieved the position he desired.

The lessee will have paid out £1,802, and he is undoubtedly entitled to a tax deduction on this. He therefore gets tax relief of £937—this being the amount which we described in the preceding paragraph as a subsidy from the Chancellor. Whereas in that paragraph the lessee's net cost after tax relief was £1,802, his net cost on the basis described in this paragraph is £865.

5.63 The third course is the one whose end result is least clear. The parties can attempt to make the payment outside the area of the payer's expense and the recipient's income. By describing it as some sort of capital payment, and by having the lessee undertake that he will not claim to deduct it, the hope is that the lessor will not be taxable on it. However many cases, of which the Falkirk Ice Rink (1975 STC 434) is a recent example, show that this is not necessarily so.

5.64 What seems to us to be necessary is an attempt to analyse the transaction concerned, and to see how it fits within the framework of the finance lease at which we have been looking. A lease is basically an agreement under which the lessor grants possession and use, and the lessee gives consideration for it in the form of rent. There are obviously refinements and exceptions, but the underlying premise must be that the payments made by the lessee are rent and as such are taxable in the lessor's hands.

If you start by trying to prove the negative, by trying to say that some payments are not taxable, that they are somehow different, then do so with your eyes open. There is no easy solution. There is not even an obviously equitable solution, because taxation is so seldom even-handed, particularly where currency movements create surpluses or income without matching deficits or expense, and vice-versa

CAPITAL ALLOWANCES FOR NON TRADING LESSOR

5.65 We will now consider the tax position of a company which engages in leasing plant as a peripheral activity—not as a part of its trade so far as the Inspector of Taxes sees that trade.

PREVIOUS LEGISLATION

5.66 Capital allowances for such a company are made available by S. 46(1) FA 1971. This is the provision which replaced S.42CAA 1968, itself the consolidation of S. 298 of the 1952 Income Tax Act.

The last section merits some examination, because subsequent changes can only be fully understood against the background of what was there before.

S. 298 ITA 1952 gave allowances to a lessor provided

a) he incurred capital expenditure on the provision of the let plant.

b) he bore the burden of the plant's wear and tear

and

c) the lessee to whom the plant was let used it in his own trade.

These requirements were matched by those of the following section, (S. 299) which gave the allowances to the lessee if he, rather than the lessor, bore the burden of wear and tear. The two sections were thus complementary: without overlap or gap between them. It was this feature of the legislation which enabled the Court of Appeal to "read into" S. 298 the third of the conditions mentioned above, even though it was only explicitly stated in S. 299 (Macsaga Investment Co. Ltd. v Lupton (44 TC 659)).

5.67 However, the very considerable difficulty in interpreting the legislation was highlighted by the Court of Appeal in the same case, when they came to consider the meaning of the words "bears the burden of wear and tear".

The circumstances were that a building was let by Macsaga to the Minister of Works. Included in the leased premises were the building's lifts, whose anticipated life was twenty five years at most, whilst the lease was for thirty five years. It was therefore probable that the lifts would need to be replaced during the lease term. The repairing covenants in the lease were such that the lessee had not only to pay for any repairs to the lifts during the lease, but also had to pay for their replacement if and when this became necessary.

On the other hand, he did not have to hand the building back to the lessor at the end of the lease with brand new lifts in it. In that sense the lessor would have suffered some wear and tear to the equipment between the dates he first made it available to the lessee and the date he got back its replacement.

5.68 In the event the Court of Appeal were split on the question what exactly was meant by bearing the burden of wear and tear, and accordingly could not agree who was the bearer, although this did not prevent their finding, unanimously, that Macsaga was disqualified from allowances because the lessee was not trading and therefore did not meet the third, implicit, requirement of S. 298.

5.69 Another case, (Lupton v Cadogan Gardens Development Ltd., 47 TC 1) similar in all respects except that the lessee was trading, was therefore taken to the Court of Appeal three years later, in 1971. The Court held that:-

a) The lessor would be left with some plant at the end of the lease, not the same plant items that he had started with, but which had suffered some wear and tear.

b) The lessor was not entitled to receive capital allowances on his expenditure on the original plant. The lessee was the person who was responsible for bearing the wear and tear on this plant, and was therefore entitled to the allowances concerned.

c) The lessee was the person who actually paid for the replacement items, and he could deduct the cost of them as a trading expense.

5.70 Lord Justice Russell did not pretend that this was anything other than an odd and illogical decision. In relation to the lessee's right to a trading deduction for the replacement plant, the reasoning seems to have been that the lessor could not get an allowance because he had not incurred the expenditure; the lessee did incur the expenditure, but not as capital expenditure, because he achieved no lasting benefit nor obtained any asset from spending the money. Similarly, in relation to the lessee's right to the allowances on the original expenditure, and the exclusion of the lessor from a claim for them, the result was admitted to be quixotic. However, Lord Russell said that it would be wrong to say "Look at this rather curious fiscal outcome. That shows that the words do not mean what they say", (47 TC 20). Words in taxing statutes mean just what they say, and those particular words had remained substantially unaltered since originally enacted in the Customs and Inland Revenue Act 1878, even though the law had several times been consolidated, and thereby effectively re-enacted, since that date.

5.71 The Macsaga and Cadogan Gardens Developments cases may have done nothing for those particular lessors, but they did highlight the absurdities of the pre-1971 legislation, and thus paved the way for the more serviceable provisions enacted in the 1971 Finance Act. We can now turn to S. 46 of that act to see just what it has preserved and what it has abolished of the previous structure.

THE CURRENT LAW

5.72 S. 46 FA 1971 contains two separate provisions, the first giving allowances to the lessor and the second giving them to the lessee. The test is, however, no longer the question of wear and tear, and allowances are given as follows:-

a) If the lessor incurs the capital expenditure, then he gets the allowance; it is deemed for this purposes that his "letting" in itself constitutes a trade, separate from any other trade he may be carrying on.

b) If the lessee is required by the terms of the lease to incur the capital expenditure, then he gets the allowance; it is necessary that the lessee be trading if he is to qualify, but provided that he is, his entitlement to an allowance is completed by the section's deeming that the plant belongs to him.

5.73 In relation to the lessor, it is worth reminding ourselves that we here dealing with the position where the lessor concerned is not engaged in a full-scale trade of leasing, but has one or more leasing operations—what we have described in paragraph 5.65 as a peripheral activity.

Under these circumstances the lessor's letting of the plant is, as we have noted, deemed to be a separate trade, deemed to commence when he first lets the plant, and deemed to cease when he permanently ceases letting. The end of a lease, and the consequent reversion of the relevant plant to the lessor, will thus be an event which involves him in a balancing adjustment only if he "permanently" ceases to let the plant at that time.

LESSEE'S POSITION UNDER REPAIRING COVENANTS

5.74 In relation to the lessee, the provisions of S. 46(2) FA 1971 apply to all leases; whether the lessor is a trading lessor or a peripheral is irrelevant.

The second arrangement is therefore of considerable importance, and needs to be examined carefully. It is radically different from what went before. It will be noticed that the Inland Revenue have now concluded that the lessee's expenditure on replacing plant, under the repairing covenants of the lease, is capital expenditure rather than being deductible.

The plant is deemed to belong to the lessee for the whole period during which he continues to use it. If he replaces it a second time, a balancing adjustment results, just as it would with plant which actually belonged to him. But when the lease comes to an end, and the plant reverts to the lessor, the lessee receives no adjustment—the lessor is then deemed to be the person who incurred the expenditure, and it is on this basis that his balancing adjustment referred to in paragraph 5.73 would be calculated.

PLANT IN DWELLING HOUSES

5.75 So far as concerns lessors engaged only peripherally in leasing, one of the restrictions embodied in the original pre-1971 legislation has been re-enacted in the new provisions. No capital allowances whatever are available on plant which is let for use in a dwelling house. This is to prevent an individual, say, from renting his central heating system from his own company at a very low rent, while the company claims capital allowances on it.

ALLOWANCES BY WAY OF DISCHARGE OR REPAYMENT OF TAX

5.76 Allowances are given to the peripheral lessor "by way of discharge of repayment of tax", (S. 48(2) FA 1971). This contrasts with the trading lessor's allowances, given as if they were a trading expense, (S. 73(2) CAA 1968), and it is important to know just what this means in practical terms for the recipient:-

a) If plant is let to a lessee who is himself trading, then all allowances on all such plant are aggregated, and are set in the first instance against rental income from all of that plant, (S. 48(2) FA 1971).

b) If the plant is not used by the lessee for trading purposes, then the allowances on it are to be set first against its own rent only, (S. 48(3) FA 1971).

c) To the extent that there is an excess of allowances over the relevant class of income in (a) or (b) above, this excess may be carried forward, being treated as if it were an allowance for the next year, (or succeeding years), so as to be available for set off against the relevant rental income. This carry forward applies for an individual lessor subject to income tax, (S. 71(1) (b) CAA 1968), and to an incorporated lessor for purposes of corporation tax (S. 74(2) CAA 1968).

SET OFF AGAINST OTHER INCOME

5.77 As an alternative to carrying forward an excess of allowances over relevant rents, the peripheral lessor may sometimes claim to set that excess off in some other way. These other ways need careful study:-

a) For *income tax purposes,* an individual may claim to set the excess allowances against his other income for the year BUT CAN ONLY DO SO IN CASES WHERE THE LESSEE USES THE LEASED ASSET FOR TRADING PURPOSES, (S. 71(1) Proviso CAA 1968 as restricted by S. 48(4) FA 1971).

b) No claim for offset against other income liable to income tax is available where the lessee does not trade.

c) For *corporation tax purposes,* provided the lessee is trading, a peripheral lessor company may claim to offset the excess allowances against other income of the period, or against any income of the immediately preceding accounting period. (S. 74(3) and (4) CAA 1968).

d) If the lessee is not trading, the offset within the year is still available as in (c) above, but the carryback is denied, (S. 48 (4) FA 1971).

NON-TRADER DOES NOT MAKE CASE VI LOSS

5.78 It is appropriate at this point to comment on a basic misconception about the availability of allowances to lessors, particularly those lessors who are individuals. It is sometimes said that if a lessor is not carrying on a full scale leasing trade, then the Inland Revenue could assess the results of what leasing activities he does engage in under Case VI rather than under Case 1, that is to say, as a "profit" but not a "trading profit".

Leasing is an activity which generates excess allowances in the early years, which have the character of tax losses. The significance of a Case VI loss, as opposed to a Case 1 loss, is that the loss can only be carried forward to be offset against future income within Case VI, and cannot be offset against other income. But the idea that leasing might be assessable under Case VI overlooks two points.

First, an activity of buying and selling cannot be assessed under Case VI. To quote the judgment in Pearn v Miller (11 TC 613): "If it is desired to tax the difference between what a man has bought goods for, or property for, and sold them for, you can only tax it in my judgment if you can say that what he did was a trade or adventure or concern in the nature of trade. I think you cannot get under Case VI a tax out of appreciation of property: you have to get it under Case I". This must apply with even greater force to leasing than to straight purchase and sale.

Secondly, the suggestion overlooks the legislation's direction that allowances be granted by reference to a deemed trade, and its specific directions as to how they are to be available. There is no question whatever of the taxpayer needing to claim that they constitute a "loss" in order to obtain them. Allowances given by discharge or repayment are completely different from a loss.

LEASING OF INDUSTRIAL BUILDINGS

5.79 We will now examine the taxation of industrial buildings leased under a tax based lease.

It should be noted that agricultural buildings also qualify for tax allowances, and under more recent legislation so do hotels. So also does expenditure incurred by any person in connection with the working of a mine, oilwell or other source of mineral deposits, on the construction of works which are likely to be of little value when then source is no longer worked. But we will concentrate on industrial buildings.

CAPITAL ALLOWANCES

5.80 Industrial buildings allowances come in the form of an initial allowance of 50%, writing down allowances of 4% per annum, and balancing adjustments on disposal.

It is convenient to look first at the requirements which must be met if a writing down allowance is to be claimable. The legislation is to be found in Ss. 1–17 CAA 1968, but it is S. 2 which provides that the allowance shall be made:-

a) to the person who is entitled to an interest in the building;

b) provided that the building is an industrial building;

and

c) provided that the interest he holds is the relevant interest in relation to the capital expenditure incurred on the building's construction.

To understand this section properly we need to define "industrial building" and "relevant interest".

DEFINITION OF INDUSTRIAL BUILDING

5.81 A building is only an industrial building if it is in use for one or more of a number of purposes specified in S. 7 CAA 1968. Shops, offices and houses are not industrial buildings. But in general it is the nature of the user's trade which determines whether a building is or is not an industrial building; the actual use of the building itself is not what S. 7 directs us to look at.

It should be also noted that allowances are only available when the building is in *use* as an industrial building. We have seen that if plant is let in the course of the trade of leasing, then the letting itself constitutes a "use" of the plant for the purposes of the trade. With buildings the position is different. Letting is not the relevant factor—the tenant's use is what matters.

DEFINITION OF RELEVANT INTEREST

5.82 The relevant interest is defined in S. 11 CAA 1968, as being the interest in the building held by the person who incurred the expenditure at the time he incurred it.

If we consider the following picture

A = **Freeholder**

Lease for 35 years

B = **Head—leaseholder**

sub lease for 35 years less 5 days

C = **Sub-tenant**

Tenancy for 5 years, renewable annually for further periods not exceeding 29 years + 355 days

D = **Sub-sub-tenant who uses, or is to use the building as an industrial building** if C incurs expenditure on constructing the building, then his sub-lease is the relevant interest so far as concerns that expenditure. He is entitled to allowances by reference to that expenditure, and that interest. If he assigns his interest to someone else, that other becomes entitled to allowances in his capacity as new owner of the relevant interest, although as we will see below, the allowances that the assignee receives are not based on the price paid by him and are not even necessarily based on the amount of the original expenditure incurred by C.

What is sometimes less than clear from textbook explanations of what is meant by "relevant interest" is that each and every one of A, B, C and D above have separate and simultaneous interests, and if any of them incurs expenditure on the construction of an industrial building, the expenditure will qualify for allowances in his hands by reference to his interest, which becomes "relevant" for that purpose. There is absolutely no reason why two or more people should not be claiming allowances at the same time for their separate amounts of expenditure on the same building. For each of them the rules are the same if their relevant interest changes hands.

5.83 If at the time the expenditure was incurred C was not only the subtenant but also the freeholder, (i.e. A and C were one and the same), then the relevant interest by reference to which A/C incurred the expenditure would be the freehold interest; S. 11(2) describes it as the interest which "is an interest which is reversionary on" the other or all the others.

If it was B who incurred the expenditure it would be his head-lease which was relevant. Although the act is silent on this question it is accepted by the Inland Revenue that B's entitlement to allowances would not be affected by the fact that C held an interest intermediate between his own interest and the sub-sub-tenant D who was the user of the building.

Going back to the assumption that C incurred the expenditure, if his interest merged with that of B, then B's interest would become the the relevant one. One occasion for merger is the expiry of

C's sub-lease at the end of 34 years and 360 days—B obtains the relevant interest for the final five days of his own lease. A more significant merger of interests would occur if C surrendered his lease to B, or if C were to acquire the interest formerly held by B.

INITIAL ALLOWANCES

5.84 Having looked at the conditions upon which writing down allowances are available, it is now appropriate to turn to initial allowances. S. 1 CAA 1968 gives an initial allowance:-

a) to the lessor who incurs capital expenditure on the construction of the building;

b) provided that the lessee who is to use the building holds a lease "to which the relevant interest is reversionary" (i.e. the lessee is the tenant, sub-tenant, sub-sub-tenant or so forth of the lessor in whose relevant interest the expenditure was incurred);

c) and provided that the building does subsequently come to be used as an industrial building by that lessee.

The initial allowance is given to the lessor for the period in which he incurs the expenditure, or in which the user's tenancy begins if that is later.

If, after the tenancy has commenced, the building is used by the tenant for a purpose which means that it fails to qualify as an industrial building, then any initial allowance which may already have been given to the lessor is withdrawn.

EXPENDITURE ON WHICH ALLOWANCES ARE BASED

5.85 So far, in reference to both writing down allowances and initial allowances we have referred to expenditure on the construction of a building which is to be an industrial building (paragraphs 5.80 and 5.84).

That is fine if the lessor does the constructing himself. It is however more likely that he will purchase a building. If he does, he needs to analyse very carefully just what he is buying.

a) It is, as we have seen, the relevant interest which he needs to acquire, if he is to inherit an entitlement to allowances from the person who did incur expenditure on construction by reference to that relevant interest.

b) This is now capable of some modest extension where the holder of the relevant interest retains that interest but grants a long lease at a premium to the person we have been referring to as the "purchaser". If the holder of the relevant interest and the purchaser make a joint election, then the purchaser's long lease becomes the relevant interest, and the previously relevant interest ceases to be the relevant interest so far as concerns the entitlement to allowances on the original construction expenditure. The person who has paid a premium for the long lease then claims allowances on the amount of that premium, or the original construction expenditure if less.

5.86 The amount upon which the purchaser thereafter obtains allowances, and the type of allowances he obtains depends upon the features of his acquisition.

a) If what he obtains is a new and unused building acquired from the person who constructed it, then his allowances are calculated under S. 5(1) CAA 1968 on the lower of

i) the price he pays for the relevant interest, (or the premium paid for the grant of the long lease of that relevant interest).

and

ii) the expenditure incurred by the person who constructed the building

b) If he obtains a new and unused building and the person from whom he acquires it is engaged in a trade of developing (that is building and selling unused) buildings which are to be used as industrial buildings, then the allowances available to the purchaser are calculated on the price he pays and the developer's expenditure is ignored.

In either event he is entitled to initial and writing down allowances on the price, premium or expenditure, that amount being regarded as having been incurred when the price or premium became payable. The price paid for the purchase of the relevant interest in either of the above cases is to be reduced in accordance with S. 17(3)CAA 1968, so that only the proportion of it relating to the industrial building is taken into account for capital allowance purposes. The intent of this section is to exclude from those allowances that part of the price related to the land itself, or to items other than industrial buildings.

5.87 If at the time of purchase, the building has already come into use as an industrial building, the purchaser would receive no initial allowance, and his annual writing down allowance (over the remainder of the building's twenty five year life) would be the lower of his purchase price or its construction cost divided by the number of years remaining. The amount might be even lower if during some part of the building's life it had not been used as an industrial building.

One's immediate reaction is to say that this is a basis so unfavourable that no lessor should be tempted to purchase relevant interets in second hand buildings. But consider the case of a factory built for £100,000 in 1963. It now has nine years left of its twenty five year life. It is not perhaps unreasonable to assume that its market value today might still be £100,000. If it changes hands now at that price, the purchaser will get allowances by reference to the original cost of construction, because the previous owner will have all his allowances withdrawn by a balancing adjustment. The purchaser will therefore get a writing down allowance of £11,111 in each of the first nine years of his ownership. It is also not unreasonable to assume that he might be able to let the building for approximately the same amount because 11% of the market value is not out of line with market conditions. He will thus achieve a tax free return of 11% on his investment, since this is the cash he receives, and the allowances eliminate his tax liability on it.

5.88 **FIXED PLANT IN INDUSTRIAL BUILDINGS**

Plant which is movable can be owned and let separately from the ownership and letting of the building in which it is located. On the other hand items which are regarded as plant for tax purposes, but which are "fixed" to a building or land become one with that land or building. Ownership of the plant, and arrangements for letting it, must therefore follow the same pattern as that of the building itself.

This means that a tenant who "fixes" plant to a building which is the property of his (freeholder) landlord fails to meet the normal ownership requirements necessary to enable him to claim plant and machinery allowances. The normal tenant is given his allowances through the back door route provided by S. 85 CAA 1968, on capital sums which he is regarded as having "contributed" towards the plant which has become owned by the freeholder. The contribution route is no longer available where tenant and landlord are connected, as a result of S. 42 FA 1976.

5.89 However the difficulty of fitting lessors into S. 85 CAA 1968 can be seen if we recognise that the lessor is in the dual situation of being a tenant of the freeholder, and is also the "landlord" of the lessee. S. 85 gives the "contributor" allowances in two circumstances:-

a) If his contribution is for the purposes of a trade carried on by him, he is to be given the allowances to which the freeholder would have been entitled had he incurred the expenditure. This is unsatisfactory because the letting of industrial buildings, with or without fixed plant inside them, cannot be a trade for tax purposes. Rental income from land and buildings is a Schedule A source, not one within Schedule D Case I.

b) If his contribution is for the purposes of a trade carried on by a tenant of land in which he has an interest, he (the holder of that interest) gets the allowances to which the freeholder would have been entitled had he (the freeholder) incurred the expenditure. Unfortunately, as we have seen in paragraphs 5.09 and 5.81, it is not plant and machinery allowances which can be given by reference to the tenant's trade, but only industrial buildings allowances.

Despite the apparent inapplicability of this legislation, (and there is an exactly parallel gap in the recent legislation concerning availability of allowances to those who pay premiums for long leases), it is understood that the Inland Revenue do grant plant and machinery allowances to lessors who fix plant into buildings which they let for use as industrial buildings provided that the lessor brings a disposal value into account when he ceases to hold the relevant interest. Exactly how he is to arrive at such a disposal value it not at all clear.

MANNER OF GIVING INDUSTRIAL BUILDINGS ALLOWANCES

5.90 Where the holder of the relevant interest in the industrial building is not himself the person who uses that building, but he lets it (directly or through one or more intermediate lessees) to a tenant who so uses it, then capital allowances are given to the relevant interest holder "by way of discharge or repayment of tax". This is the phrase we have already examined in paragraphs 5.76 and 5.77, since it is the way in which the non-trading lessor of plant and machinery is given his allowances.

In the case of industrial buildings allowances, the relief is to be given primarily against the income from the letting of all industrial buildings then being let. We have already noted in the preceding paragraph that whether or not the lessor is engaged in any other trading activities, his income from letting these buildings is taxable under Schedule A.

If the capital allowances given by way of discharge or repayment exceed the amount of the Schedule A income against which they are primarily to be set, then the excess is either available for carry forward against the same class of income in future years, or is offsettable against other income. It is interesting to note that S. 74 CAA 1968 allows an offset against other income for the year, or for the previous year, without any restriction which contrasts with the position in paragraph 5.77 where we saw certain restrictions applied for plant and machinery allowances if the lessee was not trading.

CAPITAL EXPENDITURE

5.91 We cannot leave the question of leasing industrial buildings without coming back to the problem of what expenditure can be regarded as "capital" so as to fit within the necessary conditions for allowances to become available.

In paragraph 5.14 we indicated that expenditure must fit the economic concept of fixed capital. The lessor who spends money on plant must be intending, (and subsequent events must demonstrate this intention), to make profit from "keeping" that plant, rather than from "letting it change masters". In the case of industrial buildings the underlying concept is no different, but it is even more important that the lessor fully understands its implications. These implications are now examined.

5.92 In general plant may be expected to have a useful working life of, say, between ten and twenty years. An owner who uses it himself would expect to depreciate it to a relatively small value if not to zero over its anticipated life. A lessor of plant can indubitably say that he is profiting from retaining that plant if his rent receipts recoup substantially the whole cost of the asset (and interest) over its anticipated life. Its residual value is likely to be comparatively small. There will be exceptions, but the majority of finance leases will be based on the lessor's rents forming the source of his profit, without any significant contribution from the asset's disposal proceeds at the end of the lease. We have also noted that lessors frequently accept that the greater part of such proceeds belong equitably to the lessee.

5.93 With let buildings the position is no different. If the rent receivable by the lessor is to be set to recoup him his expenditure, plus interest and profit, from retaining the buildings for their anticipated life, then his leases are going to be exceptionally long ones, compared to the duration of his plant leases. If he gives the Inland Revenue any grounds for believing that he does not intend to retain his relevant interest in the buildings, and to continue letting them to industrial users, throughout their lives, then he calls into question whether he is not in a business of profiting from interests in land and buildings by selling those interests, and whether his interests are not therefore trading stock rather than fixed capital.

For the lessor's case that he holds the assets as fixed capital to be convincing he must be careful how he finances them. The Revenue might doubt for instance whether buildings funded out of short term borrowings should be classified as fixed investments.

To help his case further, it is arguable that a lessor, who engages in plant leasing or other trading activities, should handle his industrial buildings through a separate investment company. This is not merely a matter of trying to avoid comparisons being drawn between the periods of ownership of the different classes of assets. It is rather more a matter of being able to claim that the investment company is just what it says it is, a company all of whose assets are investments. The implication of this is that the disposal of an investment cannot be a trading transaction, and that therefore the Revenue are debarred from saying that the company is turning its assets to profit by parting with them.

5.94 However, in an inflationary era, a major problem is caused because rents never do provide the lessor with substantially all of his profit; the residual value of the building will always figure significantly in the lessor's thinking. Disposing of the relevant interests, even after the end of the twenty five year life apparently envisaged for industrial buildings by S. 2 CAA 1968, can look like a trade of dealing in land.

In addition, companies in the financial leasing industry may not always feel that the very long term holding of interests in land is necessarily the way in which their funds and their expertise should be used to earn them profits. But to carve out lesser interests, carrying substantially all of the value, out of the relevant interests, and then to dispose of those lesser interests can similarly look like a trade of dealing in land.

Unfortunately there is no easy and safe way to circumvent these uncertainties.

ANTI-AVOIDANCE LEGISLATION

5.95 All anti-avoidance legislation is very complex and detailed. It is remarkably easy to assume that these anti-avoidance provisions were enacted to stop particular abuses current at the time, that the abuses are as a result no longer current and that the provisions are therefore spent. Remarkably easy, but also remarkably risky. It is equally if not more dangerous to approach the legislation attempting to discern the patterns of the transactions it sought to stop and then to measure your proposed transactions against those patterns rather than against the legislation.

Frequently the legislation is not wholly successful in preventing the avoidance arrangements at which it is aimed. As frequently it strikes at transactions at which it was not aimed. Readers ought to study the legislation itself if they want to know whether it affects them or not. However with this very strong warning ringing in our ears, we will attempt a small amount of pattern discernment. Our examination will be cursory by comparison with the depth and detail of our studies in this chapter so far.

RE-DATING OF EXPENDITURE

5.96 In S. 40(2) FA 1971 appears the first of a number of provisions designed to avoid the "redating" of expenditure. If capital expenditure had originally been incurred before 27 October 1970, the new 100% allowances would not be available. The provision is designed to stop artificial transactions between connected companies. For example it might be that the original owner of the plant had tax losses against which a balancing charge could be set, but that a connected company could benefit from the 100% allowance which it could claim under the new system if it could claim under the new system if it could purchase the plant concerned after 27 October 1970.

The new system introduced by the 1971 act was intended to encourage new investment, not to reduce tax liabilities by permitting movement of old expenditure into the new era, whether by the use of sale and leaseback techniques or by straight sale to another group company.

TRIGGERING A FIRST YEAR ALLOWANCE

5.97 Whether or not the original expenditure was incurred before 27 October 1970, and whether or not parties to the relevant transaction are connected, it is possible that a tax saving might be achieved by triggering off a first year allowance. For instance a company which could take a balancing charge without its involving an immediate tax payment, could sell its plant to another company and lease it back. The first year allowance given to that other could be seen as a direct drain on the Exchequer.

Sch. 8(3)(1)(b) FA 1971 was designed to remove that advantage, by denying a first year allowance to the lessor. By the following year it had become obvious that it was not totally effective. As originally drafted it did not prevent the granting of a first year allowance if the lease-back was being effected to a fellow subsidiary of the original owner. Nor did it work if there was some discontinuity in the use of the plant by the original owner at the time he leased it back. The law was therefore tightened in S. 68(3) FA 1972 to extend the areas in which first year allowances are denied to cover these two points.

On the other hand it was not intended that the first year allowance should be withheld in cases where the plant changes hands before it is first used for the purposes of the trade and S. 68(5) FA 1972 ensured that the first year allowance would remain available in such circumstances.

ARTIFICIALLY INCREASING THE AMOUNT ON WHICH ALLOWANCES CLAIMABLE

5.98 The effect of Sch. 8(3)(1) FA 1971 is not limited to denying first year allowances. It also attacks both vendor and purchaser if the price at which the plant changes hands is greater than the disposal value that the vendor takes into account for his balancing adjustment calculation. It will be remembered that disposal values cannot exceed the original expenditure incurred by the person whose disposal of the plant is in point, (paragraph 5.33).

What Sch. 8(3)(1) requires is that the excess of the price paid over that disposal value is to be ignored by both vendor and purchaser.

Once again the law had to be clarified a year later by S.68(4) FA 1972. No disposal value falls to be taken into account if the vendor is geographically outside the scope of UK taxes. It was therefore possible for plant to be sold into the UK from a non-resident fellow subsidiary company at an inflated price, without the excess amount being chargeable to UK tax in the vendor's hands, but with the purchaser being entitled to an allowance on the whole price supposedly paid. Similarly there is no such thing as a disposal value if plant is disposed of before it is brought into use, and this also presented an opportunity to increase its "price" artificially for capital allowances.

5.99 S. 68(4) FA 1972 introduces a considerable amendment of the earlier legislation in these circumstances. Instead of looking to that non-existent disposal value, we are instructed instead to look to the lowest of

a) the open market value of the plant

b) what the seller originally spent on it

or

c) what was spent on it by any associate of his

If we consider, for example, what would be the effect of these provisions on an item of plant originally acquired in Switzerland a few years ago by the Swiss fellow subsidiary for, say:-

1,000 Swiss Francs at the exchange rate Sw.Fr. 10 = £1 £100

The open market value of this plant may perhaps now be

800 Swiss Francs at Sw.Fr. 4 = £1 £200

It is obvious that to bring that asset into the UK tax net in any way which gets caught in Sch. 8(3)(1) can only be achieved at the expense of some considerable distortion, and that this distortion is not in this case related to any tax avoidance or its prevention.

SHIFTING ALLOWANCES OUT OF THE PUBLIC SECTOR

5.100 A whole further series of anti-avoidance sections are designed to prevent what the Revenue sees as an unjustifiable shifting of tax allowances into the profit making private sector. Capital allowances are technically available to those state and local authority enterprises which trade, and are therefore subject to tax, but most of those enterprises are unable to use their allowances because of the inadequacy of their own profits.

5.101 Where plant is leased to one of the public corporations, for instance railway engines to British Rail, allowances will obviously become available in the private sector which would not otherwise have been capable of being utilised. On the other hand, the private sector will receive a commensurate amount of taxable income in the form of rentals for the plant concerned.

If we compare the public sector's borrowing with its leasing alternative, looking at each from the viewpoint of the Inland Revenue, we see the following. (All the figures are taken from the basic data in paragraph 2.08, and it is assumed that if the public corporation borrowed to purchase its own asset, the interest charged to it would be equal to the rate implicit in the lease.)

a) Borrowing

Public corporation pays interest of £42,000 on which it receives no tax relief because of non-availability of taxable income	–
Private sector lender receives interest	£ 42,000
and itself pays interest	(33,263)
Net amount on which tax is chargeable	£ 8,737

b) Leasing

Public corporation pays rents of £142,000 on which it receives no tax relief because of non-availability of taxable income	–
Private sector lender receives rentals	£142,000
and is entitled to capital allowances	(100,000)
as well as being entitled to relief for interest	(33,263)
Net amount on which tax is chargeable	£ 8,737

This demonstrates that there is no tax advantage to be gained from leasing to public corporations other than the standard one available through all leasing, namely that capital allowances are available to reduce tax liabilities before rentals receivable create equivalent further liabilities.

THE CALL FOR SELF RESTRAINT

5.102 This acceleration of tax allowances in front of taxable income is what the financial leasing industry is all about, and in particular it is what capital allowances at their present levels are about. It would therefore be unlikely for the authorities to introduce legislation to strike at an "avoidance" which appears to be the whole purpose of the tax structure itself, despite the worries some people have. The Revenue is not concerned with preventing the leasing industry from mobilising capital allowances from industrial investment in such a way as to reduce the taxable profits of lessors in particular and the financial sector in general.

Sir William Pile, the Chairman of the Board of Inland Revenue, told the Equipment Leasing Association on 20 September 1977 that the Revenue has absolutely no animus against the established leasing industry. He went on to say, however, that there are transactions carried out under the guise of leasing by some operators, about which the Revenue feels justifiably suspicious. "A little bit of self restraint around the margins will be in everyone's interests" is the phraseology which he is quoted as having used.

There are four particular areas where self restraint was or is called for. These areas are now examined.

THE PUBLIC CORPORATIONS' LEASING DIRECTIVE

5.103 First the public corporations and local authorities could not be allowed to lease unchecked because their investment programmes were so vast that the entire "taxable capacity" of the nation could have been eliminated. It was however a simple matter for the authorities to lay down by administrative decree the occasions on which leasing was and was not appropriate. That directive has been in existence and operating smoothly for a number of years and no anti avoidance legislation has been required.

GROUP RELIEF AND PARTNERSHIP SCHEMES

5.104 The second area, and this did call for anti avoidance treatment, was the use of group relief (or partnership) arrangements rather than leasing in order to extract capital allowances from the public sector into the private. The number of variations on the single theme was large, and the legislation in Ss. 28–32 and Sch 12 FA 1973 is accordingly complex and wide ranging. It is dangerous to assume that because your own transaction is not exactly the one at which the legislation was originally aimed, it will therefore not be affected by that legislation. Provided that readers bear this in mind, we can however indicate the general form of transaction at which the legislation was aimed.

5.105 A public corporation borrowed funds from a bank or banks in the private sector. It lent those funds to its own newly formed subsidiary, which used the money to purchase plant and machinery. The subsidiary then leased that plant to its parent, the public corporation. So far so good—there is no tax avoidance involved here. The bank is receiving interest. The subsidiary is receiving capital allowances, but, as both the subsidiary and its parent are in the public sector and do not have enough profits make use of those allowances, the allowances are being wasted.

The twist in the scheme which allowed the allowances to leak out to the bank (or elsewhere in the private sector) lay in the structure of the subsidiary's share capital and ownership. In order to enable it to surrender its losses (the first year allowances) it was created a 75% subsidiary of the lending bank, so as to be within the meaning of the group relief legislaiton. Or else it was made a 90% subsidiary of a holding company which itself was owned by a consortium of private sector companies, the bank probably being one of these.

This 75% or 90% ownership could be achieved as no more than a tax technicality, owing to the way in which "subsidiary" and "ordinary share capital" were originally defined for the purposes of National Defence Contribution in the Finance Act 1938. These definitions were, until 1973, preserved unchanged in the tax legislation, (in S. 532 and S. 526(5) TA 1970 respectively). For all other purposes, including the question whether or not the company was a subsidiary of the bank for Companies Act purposes, its share capital was such that it was a member of the public corporation's group, and of no other.

5.106 Once the first year allowances had been stripped out by means of a surrender of group relief, the special shares could be sold by the bank etc. to the public corporation. That was always slightly dangerous if a bank were selling, because most of a bank's investments are current assets—and group relief could be withdrawn if the subsidiary from which it had been received turned out to be one in respect of which "a profit on a sale of the shares would be treated as a trading receipt of (the banks) trade", (S. 258 (7) TA 1970). It was less dangerous if the shares were retained but with their special rights being altered so that the company ceased to be a member of the bank's or the consortium's group.

Similar results could be achieved through partnerships of companies, with the profit sharing, (or loss sharing), arrangements being changed after the banks and their associates had had their first year allowances.

5.107 These weaknesses in the legislation were removed by the Finance Act 1973. S. 28 enacts that group losses cannot be surrendered to a "parent" merely on the strength of the technical form of the share capital. A parent needs now to be a genuine parent, by reference to entitlement to profits and to surpluses on a winding up.

S. 29 extends the restrictions in S. 28 by preventing surrenders of group relief where arrangements are in existence for a company to be moved from one group to another or for a trade to be transferred between companies. S. 30 contains restrictions where it is not the company which is to be shifted but its trade, and the contracts which it has entered into in the course of that trade. Strangely, it is not the denial of group relief which is called for in these circumstances. The restrictions take the form of denying the carry forward of losses, or their offset against other income of the year or the preceding year.

PARTNERSHIPS OF COMPANIES AND INDIVIDUALS

5.108 The third area calling for self-restraint was where a partnership consisting of a company and a number of individuals with high marginal rates of tax were so structured that the individuals were effectively "buying" from their corporate partner the benefits of first year allowances. The corporate partner might have been the only one required to put up capital to finance the leasing business of the partnership, and in that sense it would be realistic to regard the arrangement as no more than a sale by it of tax allowances to its partners.

S. 31 FA 1973 attacked the corporate partner by applying tax to the "income" he derived from selling allowances, and prevening him from offsetting other losses against that income.

The law was considerably strengthened by S. 41 FA 1976 which prevents an individual from setting his tax losses against his other income where those tax losses emanate from a partnership of which a company is or is to be a partner. The section also cuts away the advantages which could previously be derived by an individual from partnership operations or transfers of assets to associates where "a scheme has been effected ... such that the sole or main benefit that might be expected to accrue ... was the obtaining of a reduction in tax liability". We will examine the phrase "sole or main benefit" further in paragraph 5.114, but we would point out at this stage that it is probably less difficult to use against individuals than against companies engaged in a trade of leasing.

THE QUESTIONS RAISED BY CAR LEASING

5.109 We said in paragraph 5.102 that there were four areas in which the Revenue appeared to think that self restraint by lessors was advisable. Two of these, the group relief arrangements and the company partnership arrangements have now been covered in the anti-avoidance legislation at which we have been looking. Another, straightforward public sector leasing, has been controlled by administrative direction.

The fourth area which has not been specifically legislated against relates to car leasing. We will now examine what action might be open to the Revenue, even without a change in the law, if a lessor were to push each of the elements of a finance lease to, or beyond, the limits of credibility.

Let us assume for instance that a business obtains, by leasing, a car for the use of an employee, and that at least 10% of the car's use is for business purposes. Let us assume also that the car is an expensive one, but that the leasing company writes what is a full payout lease for a term of only two years. At the end of that lease term the lessor sells the car to the same employee for a fraction of its open market value at that time.

5.110 It is said that under existing law:-

a) The business is entitled to deduct over the two year term the whole of the rents it pays; not only is there no restriction under Sch. 8(12) FA 1971 for the reasons explained in paragraph 5.26 but nothing prevents the lessee from deducting a rent so calculated as to write off the whole cost of the car over two years. The lessee himself gets no benefit from the residual value of the car; that value has not been allowed for in setting the level of the rents, and nor does the lessee receive any amount "by way of rebate of hire".

b) The employee is taxable only on a "benefit" quantified at the normal scale figures set out in Sch. 7 FA 1976 in respect of the availability of the car. He does not get taxed on any benefit deemed to arise from his purchase of the car at less than its open market value.

c) If the employer wished to repeat the operation in two years time with a new leased car, the employee might want to sell the first one and the gain would be free not only of capital gains tax but also of any other tax.

POSSIBLE CHALLENGES FOR LESSEE AND EMPLOYEE

5.111 From what has been said so far about Revenue and Treasury attitudes, it will be clear to readers that these problems are "political" as much as "tax technical". We would not, against that background, say that any of the above steps is free from doubt Two areas affecting respectively the lessee's and the employee's tax positions are possible lines of a relatively technical Inland Revenue attack.

a) Is there not some "duality" of purpose apparent in the lessee's paying so high a rent—is it paid "wholly and exclusively", (S. 130 TA 1970), for possession and use of the car, or is it paid in part for some other promised benefit to be derived by someone other than the lessee? If there is any such duality of purpose, the lessee loses his right to the **total** deduction (not just a proportionate part of the amount he claims to deduct).

b) It seems probable that the courts could interpret the "nomination" of the employee as purchaser as giving him a benefit taxable as income. The employer is not completey unconnected with this nomination, and that nomination is not completely unconnected with the employment contract. Also or alternatively, if he purchases the car intending to sell it he can also be taxed on the profit from this "adventure in the nature of trade".

5.112 POSSIBLE CHALLENGE FOR THE LESSOR

But there is another line of attack available, this time against the lessor. How clear is it that his original purchase of the car is capital expenditure? We have looked at this in paragraphs 5.14 to 5.20 and again in paragraphs 5.91 to 5.94. The economic meaning of retaining an asset in order to profit from its continuing power to generate income does seem hard to square with an arrangement under which our expensive and long-lasting car is "sold" over a two year period. If the lessor has not incurred capital expenditure, then a number of disasters follow so far as he is concerned:

a) He fails to get his capital allowances.

b) Although the car may be stock-in-trade, it does not qualify for stock relief, being an item let on hire, (Sch. 5 (29) (2) (c) FA 1976).

c) On a sale of an item of trading stock at a fraction of its open market price he may well be forced to bring in for tax purposes that full price in place of the nominal amount received. He would do well to consider the case of Petrotim Securities Ltd. v Ayres (41 TC 389) and in particular the dictum of

Lord Denning that the principle derived from the earlier case of Sharkey v Wernher (36 TC 275), "applies to any case where a trader may, for no reason, choose to give things away or to throw them into the sea. So when he puts securities through his books at a derisory price, the figures are to be regarded as struck out for tax purposes: and in their place you must put in the realisable market value at the time".

INLAND REVENUE ARE NOT ATTACKING THE FINANCIAL LEASING INDUSTRY

5.113 In concluding this chapter we would, however, reiterate what we said in paragraph 5.102. The Revenue is not concerned with attacking the whole tax benefit basis of leasing and in this respect we would like to debunk two baseless suggestions.

The first suggestion is that a lessor who writes substantially tax based leases is engaged in a trade of receiving rents; and in the course of that trade, he pays interest on the funds borrowed to purchase the asset concerned. He also benefits to a substantial extent from the tax reliefs which change the whole shape of his cash flow and can generally be expected to turn what would otherwise be a loss into a profit—but these group relief payments are not a part of its trade.

It is therefore said that the trade itself, rents less interest, is not being carried on a commercial basis and with a view to profit. That S. 177(4) TA 1970 therefore applies, and prevents the lessor's losses from being available for group relief purposes.

However, advice of counsel suggests that this reasoning is wrong, and there is in any event no indication whatever that the Inland Revenue think that it is in any way valid.

5.114 The second suggestion is based on the width of the wording of Sch. 8(3)(1)(c) FA 1971. This paragraph is designed to withhold first year allowances from those companies for whom "it appears that ..... the sole or main benefit ..... was the obtaining of an allowance under Chapter I of Part III of this Act". The allowances referred to are all the allowances at which we have been looking, first year, writing down and balancing adjustments.

It is therefore said that the comparison which is called for is that of the lessor's result if it received allowances in contrast with its results if no allowances were given. If the results with allowances were a profit of £100 and the results without allowances a profit of £49 or less, then the "main" benefit would appear to be the allowances—at least in the sense that the main part of the profit results therefrom.

An alternative comparison, but one which does not seem to fit the words of the act any better, would be to measure the rent which the lessor needs to charge if it received allowances with the amount of rent needed to maintain the implicit rate in the absence of those allowances.

Once again, although the applicability or otherwise of the "sole or main benefit" test for lessor companies is difficult to assess, there seems to be no indication that the Inland Revenue think that either of these two suggested comparisons should be used as a basis for withdrawing the allowances.

INLAND REVENUE PRESS RELEASE—26th JULY 1978

5.115 After the authors had completed their work on this book, the Inland Revenue issued a press release dated 26th July 1978. The text of this is reproduced below, without further comment being called for.

CAR LEASING SCHEMES

1. Many enquiries have been received from accountants and others about certain new forms of car leasing. This press release outlines the Inland Revenue's views on the tax consequences of such leases.

2. Car leases usually run for two or three years, and the rentals payable take into account an estimate of the market value of the car at the end of the lease. Under traditional contracts of this kind, the car is normally sold on the open market at the end of the lease.

Leases often provide that any excess of the sale proceeds over the anticipated residual value on which the rentals were based is to be divided between the lessor and the lessee, the greater part going to the lessee as a rebate of rentals. If, on the other hand, the car realises less than the anticipated residual value, the lessee is required to make good the shortfall by an additional rental payment.

3. The tax effects of such leases normally raise no problems. By the end of the lease the lessor has been allowed tax relief for the actual depreciation he has borne, taking into account the net proceeds of the sale of the car. The lessee is given relief on the net rentals he has paid, taking into account any rebate he receives, or shortfall he has to pay, on the disposal of the car.

4. The leases with which this notice is concerned involve some variations from the traditional provisions of car leases described above. The rentals are normally calculated by reference to a residual value which is lower than the expected open market value of the car at the end of the lease, and the car is then sold at that price to a person connected with the lessee, instead of being sold on the open market and at the open market price. The person connected with the lessee thus acquires a car for less than its market value.

5. There are many variations on this basic pattern. For instance, the residual value of the car used in calculating the rentals may be purely nominal, or may be simply a conservative estimate of the market value. The lease itself may provide for the sale of the car to a nominee of the lessee, or the car may pass through several hands before reaching the person connected with the lessee.

6. Taxation provisions not normally relevant to traditional leases may need to be considered in connection with leases of this kind. So far as the lessor is concerned, it may be appropriate to regard the car as stock-in-trade rather than an asset qualifying for capital allowances. If capital allowances are given, the provisions of Section 44 (6)(b) Finance Act 1971 may require the open market value of the car to be brought into the taxation computation at the end of the lease rather than the sale proceeds. The lessee's rental

payments may be disallowed, in whole or in part, under Section 130(a) or Section 130(f) Income and Corporation Taxes Act 1970 as not being made wholly and exclusively for the purposes of the business or as being in part capital expenditure. The person connected with the lessee who acquires the car may be liable under the provisions of Schedule E on any benefit he obtains, or under Section 492 et seq Income and Corporation Taxes Act 1970 if the car is sold. The taxation adjustments required in any particular case will depend on its circumstances.

7. Inspectors of Taxes have been given advice on dealing with leasing arrangements of this kind, and will be making enquiries and seeking adjustments as necessary when dealing with taxpayers whose liabilities are, or may be, affected. Where a taxpayer cannot reach agreement with the Inspector of Taxes about his liability, the usual rights of appeal will be available.

CHAPTER 6 – LEASING OUTSIDE THE UNITED KINGDOM

Contents

INTRODUCTION

6.01 Leasing has been used in the United States for much longer than in the UK. As a result the Americans have developed detailed accounting regulations for leasing. Other countries have on the whole not developed sophisticated rules for accounting for leasing, as their own leasing industries are relatively smaller. Tentative steps are being taken in some of these countries towards formulating draft rules, but these are as yet still at the development stage. South Africa has just published a code of leasing, but this is concerned with business practice, rather than accounting. So far as accounting rules are concerned, Canada is advancing: the Canadian Institute of Chartered Accountants published an exposure draft entitled "Accounting for Leases" in January 1978. This exposure draft is not significantly different, either in principle or in detail, from its American precursor. The remainder of this chapter is therefore devoted to the position in the United States.

LEASING IN THE U.S.

6.02 Leasing has been used extensively by American companies, both as an aid to selling a company's own products and as a means of obtaining alternative medium and long term finance. The investment tax credit has acted as an incentive to leasing. This allows the lessor to reduce his tax liability by a proportion, currently 10% of the capital expenditure. Accelerated depreciation allowances are also available for tax purposes, and it is also possible in some circumstances for the investment tax credit to be passed to the lessee.

HISTORY OF LEASE ACCOUNTING RULES

6.03 Rules covering accounting for leases have been in existence in the US for a long time. The earliest of these was issued in 1964 by the

Accounting Principles Board, (APB), the body of the American Institute of Certified Public Accountants then responsible for setting accounting standards. The APB has now been replaced as the standard-setting authority by an independent body, The Financial Accounting Standards Board (FASB). In November 1976 FASB issued the Statement of Financial Accounting Standards No. 13 (FAS 13) entitled "Accounting for Leases". This represented both a consolidation of existing pronouncements on lease accounting and an extention of them, namely a radical rethink of the principles. It applies both to lessor and lessee. It remains the authoritative work on lease accounting in the US, compliance with which is required in all financial statements purporting to be in accordance with US generally accepted accounting principles. Transitional provisions permit businesses to fall into line with certain of the requirements over a period of time up to 1980. The principal features of FAS 13 are outlined in the following paragraphs.

STATEMENT OF FINANCIAL ACCOUNTING STANDARDS No. 13

6.04 Under FAS 13 lessors and lessees must distinguish between finance and operating leases with no distinction being drawn between leasing and hire purchase. Where a lease transfers substantially all of the benefits and rights connected with the ownership of property (i.e. a finance lease) the lease is known as a "capital" lease by the lessee and either a "direct financing" or a "sales-type" lease by the lessor. All other leases are categorised as operating leases. If the lease is a capital lease it must be accounted for as the acquisition of assets by the lessee with a corresponding liability to the supplier.

THE LESSEE–DISTINGUISHING CAPITAL AND OPERATING LEASES

6.05 The lessee must decide whether his lease is a capital or operating lease. A capital lease is one which meets one of the following criteria:-

a) ownership of the property is transferred to the lessee by the end of the lease term.

b) There is an option to purchase the property at a bargain price.

c) The lease term is equal of 75% or more of the estimated economic life of the property.

d) The present value of minimum lease payments is equal to 90% or more of the fair value of the leased property, after deducting any investment tax credit retained by the lessor.

Any other lease is an operating lease.

THE LESSEE–ACCOUNTING FOR CAPITAL LEASES

6.06 The lessee's accounting treatment for a capital lease is to record a fixed asset and an equivalent liability at the present value, or fair value if less, of the minimum lease payments. The discount rate to be used in ascertaining the present value is the cost of borrowing similar funds, unless the lessee can ascertain that the implicit rate used by the lessor is lower; if he can ascertain the implicit rate is lower, he is required to use that rate. The asset is depreciated in the usual manner, and each rental payment is apportioned as partly representing repayment of capital and partly interest, so as to produce a constant rate of interest on the outstanding "liability". In the example that follows we assume that the lessee has a capital lease with annual rental payments of $28,400 per annum over a five year period and that the cost of borrowing similar funds is 13%.

EXAMPLE OF CAPITAL LEASE

6.07

	Profit & Loss	Asset	Liability
Present value at 13% of five annual rental payments of $28.400 at commencement		$99.891	$ 99,891
1st year depreciation	$ 19,978	19,978	
Interest: 13% on 99.891	12,985		
Balance (28.400–12.985)			15.415
	32.963	79,913	84.476
2nd year depreciation	19.978	19.978	
Interest: 13% on 84.476	10,982		
Balance (28.400–10.982)			17.418
	30.960	59,935	67.058
3rd year depreciation	19.978	19.978	
Interest: 13% on 67.058	8.717		
Balance (28.400–8.717)			19.683
	28.695	39.957	47.375
4th year depreciation	19.978	19.978	
Interest: 13% on 47.375	6.158		
Balance (28.400–6.158)			22.242
	26.136	19.979	25.133
5th year depreciation	19,979	19,979	
Interest: 13% on 25.133	3.267		
Balance (28.400–3.267)			25.133
	$ 23.246		
Total	$142.000		

THE LESSEE–ACCOUNTING FOR OPERATING LEASES

6.08 For leases classifed by a lessee as operating leases, the lease payments are written off to income as incurred. This is simple off-balance sheet financing. Where leases have non-cancellable terms in excess of one year, disclosure is also required by way of note to the accounts of the minimum future rental payments, both in aggregate, and for each of the following five years.

THE LESSOR–DISTINGUISHING BETWEEN DIRECT FINANCING AND SALES-TYPE LEASES AND OPERATING LEASES

6.09 Let us now turn to the lessor's accounting treatment. He is similarly required to distinguish between finance leases, (known either as direct financing leases or as sales-type leases), and operating leases, The terminology of FAS 13 is direct financing lease, not direct finance lease, and this is defined as one which meets at least one of the criteria for a capital lease set out in paragraph 6.05 above, and where additionally:-

a) the collectibility of the minimum lease payments is reasonably assured (a normal doubtful debt provision not being regarded as an indication to the contrary). Once again collectibility is the terminology used in FAS 13, denoting the view taken whether the debt is good, doubtful or bad.

and

b) there are no major uncertainties surrounding the amount of unrecoverable costs yet to be incurred by the lessor.

A sales-type lease is a direct financing lease which results in a manufacturing or dealing profit to the lessor. For the lessor, any other lease is an operating lease.

ACCOUNTING FOR DIRECT FINANCING LEASES

6.10 The accounting treatment for a direct financing lease is to record the minimum lease payments, representing the gross investment in the lease, as a debtor. The excess of this figure over the cost of the asset is recorded as unearned income and deducted from the debtor for balance sheet purposes. Over the lease term, this unearned income is required to be brought in to the income statement so as to produce a constant rate of return on the net investment in the lease, (net investment being gross investment less unearned income). However, an amount of unearned income may be released in the initial period to match initial direct costs. There is also a requirement for annual review of the residual value.

ACCOUNTING FOR SALE-TYPE LEASES

6.11 The accounting for a sales-type lease is similar to that for a direct financing lease, except that the cost of the asset will be replaced by the present value of the minimum lease payments calculated by using the interest rate implicit in the lease. This present value will be recorded as the sales value of the product and will thus determine the manufacturing or dealing profit, or loss, for the lessor.

Let us assume that the cash price of an asset which is to be leased out under a direct financing lease is $99,600. (If the lease were a sales-type lease, this price might be a manufacturing cost of $93,000 plus a profit of $6,600, this latter figure being arrived at as the difference between the present value of the minimum lease rentals, discounted at 13%, and the manufacturing cost). Let us also assume that initial direct costs of $328 have been incurred, and that these are to be covered by releasing an equivalent amount of income out of the first rental payment.

We show the gross debit and credit as they appear in the lessor's books. The income released into his profit and loss account each year is the same as the amount which in the year concerned is debited against the liability. We also show the net amount which appears in his balance sheet as a debtor. The net income recognised is $13,276, $10,982, $8,717, $6,158 and $3,267 in the five years of the lease term.

EXAMPLE OF DIRECT FINANCING, OR SALES-TYPE, LEASE

6.12

	Debit	Credit	Net: Shown in balance sheet
Cash price of asset, in case of direct financing lease	$ 99,600		
Excess of total lease payments	42,400		
"Debtor"	142,000		
"Unearned income"		42,400	
"Net investment"			99,600
1st year rent received:	28,400		
Income release for direct costs		328	
13% on 99,600		12,948	
Balance (28,400–13,276)			15,124
	113,600	29,124	84,476
2nd year rent received:	28,400		
13% on 84.476		10,982	
Balance (28.400–10,982)			17,418
	85,200	18,142	67,058
3rd year rent received:	28,400		
13% on 67,058		8,717	
Balance (28,400–8,717)			19,683
	56,800	9,425	47,375
4th year rent received:	28,400		
13% on 47,375		6,158	
Balance (28,400–6,158)			22,242
	28,400	3,267	25,133
5th year rent received:	28,400		
13% on 25,133		3,267	
Balance (28,400–3,267)			25,133

ACCOUNTING FOR OPERATING LEASES

6.13 For leases classified by a lessor as operating leases, the accounting treatment prescribed by FAS 13 is to classify the leased property as a fixed asset and depreciate it in the normal way. Rent is recorded as income, and is normally credited in level amounts through the lease term, even if it is to be received in the form of step or balloon rentals. Initial direct costs are to be deferred and spread over the lease term on the same basis as rental income. Additional disclosure is again required where operating leases contain non-cancellable terms exceeding one year—a note to the financial statements must disclose the aggregate of minimum future rentals, and the amounts for each of the succeeding five years.

THE IMPLICATIONS OF FAS 13

6.14 What, then, are the implications in practice of the requirements for the lessor and the lessee? For the lessee, FAS 13 represented a significant departure from previous practice, by requiring the majority of leases to be capitalised in the balance sheet. The financing of fixed assets using funds from external sources is widespread and entirely desirable, but off-balance sheet financing, a subtly different process which involves showing no asset and no liability, is regarded by some lessees not only as appropriate but advantageous. There is considerable disagreement, both in the US and the UK, whether capitalisation of leases should be made mandatory. The attempt in the US to specify those types of leases which must be capitalised has led to a demand for leases which fall just outside the technical rules laid down. If they do, they may well fall outside the classification of direct financing, or sales-type leases in the accounts of the lessor—a result which most lessors find undesirable.

CONSISTENCY OF TREATMENT BY LESSOR AND LESSEE

6.15 The philosophy of FAS 13 is an attempt to ensure mirror image treatment for the lessor and lessee. The criteria are therefore as similar as possible for both. However, there are certain areas, for instance collectibility of the lease payments by the lessor, where differing judgements may be made. As another example it is not normally possible for the lessee to know the interest rate implicit in the lease for the lessor. Even where he does, that rate will not often be less than his own borrowing cost unless significant tax relief obtained by the lessor is being passed on to him. Therefore, the lessee will frequently if not invariably use his own borrowing rate to ascertain the deemed cost of the leased asset and all of his figures may differ very significantly from those used by the lessor.

6.16 On balance, however, despite the potential problems mentioned in the two preceding paragraphs, it is apparent that in the vast majority of cases the treatment afforded to a lease by a lessor will be consistent with that used by a lessee. This represents a major step forward. It contrasts with the situation in the UK, where the lessee generally accounts off-balance sheet and the lessor, with tax considerations prominently in mind, treats the asset as a fixed asset. In addition the timing of income recognition from that asset and the amount at which it is stated, vary considerably depending upon the choice of accounting method. Consequently there is little consistency of treatment in the accounts of UK lessor and lessee.

6.17 From the viewpoint of the lessor the classification of leases under FAS 13 is more clear cut than previously. Since a constant rate of return on the net investment in the lease is required, most US lessors use either the rule of 78 or its more sophisticated alternative the annuity method to calculate income release. It is noteworthy that FAS 13 does not permit the investment tax credit to enter into these calculations. Therefore, the investment period method is not permissible under generally accepted accounting principles.

LEASES WITH AN OPTION TO PURCHASE

6.18 There is no distinction under US accounting rules between hire purchase and leasing, although the lessor must retain some interest in the residual value of the asset in order to qualify for the investment tax credit. Many of the situations coming within the criteria for a capital lease would be classified in the UK as hire purchase and accounted for accordingly. How UK law differentiates hire purchase from leasing transactions is discussed further in chapter 7 below.

SHOULD WE FOLLOW WHERE FAS 13 LEADS?

6.19 The main emphasis of statements on accounting principles in the US is to formulate a set of rules against which every situation can be judged. FAS 13 follows this pattern—the text runs to 40 pages and the appendices a further 75. But it would be out of line with current thinking in the UK to attempt to formulate leasing rules going into as much detail. We have already shown that if the users of financial statements in the UK are to obtain information which is comparable between different companies, then there is a need for the kind of differentiation that currently exists in the US, but this should be by broad guidelines rather than comprehensive regulations.

CHAPTER 7 – HIRE PURCHASE AND CREDIT SALE

Contents

INTRODUCTION

7.01 Hire purchase contracts and credit sale arrangements are very similar, but there are a number of basic differences between them on the one hand and leasing on the other. This chapter explores those differences, and also looks at the methods of accounting appropriate for the hire purchaser and the hire vendor.

HIRE PURCHASE DEFINED

7.02 Hire purchase, strictly speaking is a term used to describe certain types of hiring contracts in which the hirer has an option, after paying a specified number of instalments, to purchase the asset for a specified figure, this usually only being a nominal amount. If the total consideration is £5,000 or more the contract is outside the scope of hire purchase as that term is legally defined. Below the figure of £5,000 the lease with an option for the lessee to purchase the asset will come within the hire purchase laws. The significance of this is that:-

a) The law contains a number of rules to protect consumers from high-pressure salesmanship and from unwarranted repossession of the goods. Repossession ceases to be a remedy available to the vendor after a specified number of payments has been made.

b) The government uses the supply of credit through hire purchase as an economic regulator in controlling the economy. In times of reining back demand, the amounts required as initial deposits are increased and the periods over which the contract is allowed to stretch are shortened.

However, in this chapter the phrase "hire purchase" is used in a loose sense, and is taken to cover all those leases with an option given to the purchaser to acquire title during or after the lease period.

CREDIT SALE DEFINED

7.03 Credit sale differs from hire purchase in that title passes to the purchaser immediately. The vendor has no repossession rights, his only claim against the purchaser being for payment of the instalments, unless he reserves title in accordance with the Romalpa decision.

THE PASSING OF TITLE

7.04 In all cases the purchaser obtains possession and use of the asset from the start of the contract, and the passing of title is a legal nicety which does not substantially affect any of the parties except in the case of a breach of the contract terms.

DIFFERENTIATING LEASING FROM HIRE PURCHASE AND CREDIT SALE IN TAX LAW

7.05 The legal nicety of title is, for tax, the matter which makes hire purchase and credit sale significantly different from leasing. The practical consequence of this differentiation is the treatment of capital allowances. It is the purchaser who is entitled to allowances on an asset acquired by hire purchase or credit sale, whereas the lessor takes the allowances in a leasing situation.

7.06 The picture, as seen by those responsible for the tax legislation, is as follows:-

a) A leased asset is one which the owner retains, and one from which he derives his profit by retention. It is his "capital" in the economic sense of the word. Similarly, the payments made by the lessee for its use are "expense", and cannot be regarded as "acquisition costs".

b) There is therefore no way, without upsetting the whole concept of capital and income upon which our tax system is based, that capital allowances could be given to the lessee.

c) There is also no way in which the lessor can be allowed to regard the asset as other than "capital"; the way in which he earns his income from it, not the nature of the asset itself, requires this.

7.07 On the other hand, if the owner of an asset makes his profit from it by parting with it, it is "stock". This is so whether the vendor sells it outright, on credit, or by means of a hiring contract with an option granted to the hirer to purchase. The vendor cannot regard the asset as capital, whatever its nature. The very fact that he is selling or intends to sell to make his profit, demonstrates that it is stock.

Whether or not it is capital in the hands of the purchaser depends solely on what he does with it. But hire purchase and credit sale do carry at least some implication that the assets concerned are of a type which the purchaser is likely to retain for some period, not to sell immediately, and are therefore likely to be capital.

DIFFERENCES OF COMMERCIAL PRACTICE

7.08 There are other differences apart from the question of title, between the two types of transaction which are matters of commercial practice:-

a) In hire purchase and credit sale contracts the vendor has no interest in the residual value of the asset at the time the purchaser exercises his option—assuming that is that he does exercise it, and all hire purchase contracts are written on that assumption.

   In leasing, as we have seen, the lessor has some interest, even if he agrees to pass a percentage of the asset's disposal proceeds to the lessee as rebate of hire.

b) Hire purchase and credit sale contracts seldom contain any clauses under which the instalments can be adjusted for changes in interest rates, or in the rate of corporation tax.

THE VENDOR'S ACCOUNTING FOR HIRE PURCHASE

7.09 The vendor normally takes credit for income from a hire purchase "sale" on a rule of 78 basis. This can be illustrated by looking at the entries in his books.

He sets up the full amount of the instalments as a debt owed to him by the hirer, credits the cost of the asset sold to "contracts written" and credits the balance to "unearned income".

Each of the last two accounts requires some explanation. Contracts written is the equivalent of sales, except that it contains no element of profit. It needs to appear in the vendors profit and loss account, (or more strictly his trading account), if he is to produce a correct figure for turnover. But it is only a part of that turnover figure.

The balance of turnover is the amount described above as unearned income. This is released into income, (and into turnover), during the hire period. The amounts to be released in each year are derived from the sum of the quarterly digits—the proportions are 74:58:42:26:10, (see paragraph 2.47).

7.10 Taking the basic data originally set out in paragraph 2.07, with the addition of a £1 option price, we would find the following entries in the vendor's accounts.

	Contracts Written	Unearned Income	Debtor
Commencement	£100,000 CR	£42,000 CR	£142,000 DR
	Profit & Loss		
Year 1 Cash received			28,400 CR
Income release (74/210 x 42,000)	£ 14,800	14,800 DR	
End year 1	£ 14,800	27,200 CR	113,600 DR
Year 2 Cash received			28,400 CR
Income release (58/210 x 42,000)	£ 11,600	11,600 DR	
End year 2	£ 11,600	15,600 CR	85,200 DR
Year 3 Cash received			28,400 CR
Income release (42/210 x 42,000)	£ 8,400	8,400 DR	
End year 3	£ 8,400	7,200 CR	56,800 DR
Year 4 Cash received			28,400 CR
Income release (26/210 x 42,000)	£ 5,200	5,200 DR	
End year 4	£ 5,200	2,000 CR	28,400 DR
Year 5 Cash received			
Income release (10/210 x 42,000)	£ 2,000	2,000 CR	28,400 CR
Option price	1		
End year 5	£ 2,001	–	–

THE VENDOR–PROFIT AND LOSS ACCOUNT AND BALANCE SHEET

7.11 The vendor's profit and loss account and balance sheet would therefore show

Profit and Loss	Year 1	Year 2	Year 3	Year 4	Year 5	Total
Income release	£ 14,800	£11,600	£ 8,400	£ 5,200	£ 2,000	£ 42,000
Option price					1	1
Interest	(12,178)	(9,786)	(7,039)	(3,888)	(372)	(33,263)
	2,622	1,814	1,361	1,312	1,629	8,738
Doubtful debts	(864)	168	200	232	264	–
	£ 1,758	£ 1,982	£ 1,561	£ 1,544	£ 1,893	£ 8,738
Balance sheet at end of year						
Debtor	£113,600	£85,200	£56,800	£28,400	–	
Less unearned income set off	27,200	15,600	7,200	2,000	–	
	86,400	69,600	49,600	26,400	–	
Doubtful debts	864	696	496	264	–	
	£ 85,536	£68,904	£49,104	£26,136	–	

The figures themselves are of course different by only £1 from those in paragraph 2.50 although their presentation demonstrates that the transaction is not quite the same as a finance lease.

7.12 The vendor, as we have seen, normally releases income into his profit and loss account during the hire period using the rule of 78 as his guideline. This is the accounting method recommended for his use by the Institute of Chartered Accountants in England and Wales. (Members Handbook, Section N 23).

THE HIRER'S ACCOUNTING

7.13 The hirer, on the other hand, by convention capitalises the asset and uses an annuity calculation to determine how much of each instalment represents the "interest" on his borrowing. In doing his sums he is not inconvenienced by any difficulties over discovering the implict rate of return, because hire purchase law compels the vendor to disclose a cash price as well as quoting the hire purchase terms.

THE HIRER—PROFIT AND LOSS ACCOUNT

7.14 The hirer generally capitalises the asset at its cash price, sets up the full amount of the instalments as a liability to the vendor, and carries the balancing debit as an "interest suspense account". Using the calculations in paragraph 2.36 his accounts should look like this

	Profit & Loss	Liability	Interest Suspense	Fixed Asset
Commencement		£142,000 Cr	£42,000 Dr	£100,000 Dr
Year 1 Depreciation	£20,000			20,000 Cr
Interest on £100,000	12,955		12,955 Cr	
Cash paid		28,400 Dr		
End year 1	£32,955	£113,600 Cr	£29,045 Dr	£ 80,000 Dr
Year 2 Depreciation	£20,000			£ 20,000 Cr
Interest on £84,555	10,954		10,954 Cr	
Cash paid		28,400 Dr		
End year 2	£30,954	£ 85,200 Cr	£18,091 Dr	£ 60,000 Dr
Year 3 Depreciation	£20,000			£ 20,000 Cr
Interest on £67,109	8,694		8,694 Cr	
Cash paid		28,400 Dr		
End year 3	£28,694	56,800 Cr	9,397 Dr	40,000 Dr
Year 4 Depreciation	£20,000			20,000 Cr
Interest on £47,403	6,141		6,141 Cr	
Cash paid		28,400 Dr		
End year 4	£26,141	£ 28,400 Cr	£ 3,256 Dr	£ 20,000 Dr
Year 5 Depreciation	£20,000			£ 20,000 Cr
Interest on £25,144	3,256		3,256 Cr	
Cash instalment		28,400 Dr		
option **option**	1			
End year 5	£23,257	—	—	—

THE HIRER—BALANCE SHEET

7.15 The normal figures at which asset and liability are shown in the hirer's balance sheet are as follows:

End of:	**Year 1**	**Year 2**	**Year 3**	**Year 4**	**Year 5**
Fixed Asset net of depreciation	£80,000	£60,000	£40,000	£20,000	—
Hire purchase creditor	113,600	85,200	56,800	28,400	—
Interest suspense	29,045	18,091	9,397	3,256	—
	£84,555	£67,109	£47,403	£25,144	£ —

The interest suspense debtor can either be shown among other debtors in the balance sheet, or can be deducted, as above, from the hire purchase creditor. The hire purchase creditor is usually included with creditors generally (whether or not net of interest suspense).

It is possible, as an alternative, to deduct the net creditor from the fixed asset—this could clearly not be done on the figures set out above, and is not a method to be recommended.

COMPARISON WITH U.S. PRACTICE

7.16 The hire purchase accounting methods illustrated above are broadly similar to those used in the US for finance leases. The US treatment has been examined in chapter 6 and the lack of differentiation between the purchase option contracts and those without the option has been pointed out.

The distinction in the UK is based on the taxation theory that the former is a method of getting rid of the asset and the latter a design for retaining it—and that the interests of the lessor and those of the hire-vendor in the asset are accordingly entirely different.

SUBSTANCE AND FORM

7.17 In our view this differentiation obscures rather than illuminates the true and fair view which the accounts should show.

We would do well to bear in mind that the Statement of International Accounting Standards No. 1 requires that substance be accounted for where form and substance differ.

Is substance sufficiently different to justify the finance lessor showing in his balance sheet a fixed asset which the vendor would not show if the transaction were one of hire purchase? Is the position of the lessee in a full pay out lease so different from that of the hire purchaser that the former should expense his rents while the latter capitalises the asset and reflects the funding of it? How much substance does that purchase option really have?

The authors rest their case. They suggest that the answers to these questions are self-evident.

APPENDIX

Contents

TABLE A – See paragraph 3.59

		Rent receivable immediately before beginning of quarter	Outstanding borrowing at beginning of quarter	Interest payable at end of quarter	Outstanding borrowing at end of quarter
Year 1	Q1	£(7,100)	92,900	3,251	96,151
	Q2	(7,100)	89,051	3,117	92,168
	Q3	(7,100)	85,068	2,977	88,045
	Q4	(7,100)	80,945	2,833	83,778
				£12,178	
Year 2	Q1	(7,100)	76,678	2,684	79,362
	Q2	(7,100)	72,262	2,529	74,791
	Q3	(7,100)	67,691	2,369	70,060
	Q4	(7,100)	62,960	2,204	65,164
				£ 9,786	
Year 3	Q1	(7,100)	58.064	2,323	60,387
	Q2	(7,100)	53,287	2,131	55,418
	Q3	(7,100)	48,318	1,933	50,251
	Q4	(7,100)	43,151	1,726	44,877
				£ 8,113	
Year 4	Q1	(7,100)	37,777	1,511	39,288
	Q2	(7,100)	32,188	1,287	33,475
	Q3	(7,100)	26,375	1.055	27,430
	Q4	(7,100)	20,330	813	21,143
				£ 4,666	
Year 5	Q1	(7,100)	14,043	562	14.605
	Q2	(7,100)	7,505	300	7,805
	Q3	(7,100)	705	29	734
	Q4	(7,100)	(6,366)	(159)	(6,525)
				732	
Year 6			Tax	3,393	(3,132)

Non-tax based lease
Interest payable 3½% per quarter for first two years, then rising to 4% per quarter for remainder of lease

	Pre-tax	Post-tax
Cash flow has changed from positive	£ 8,737	£ 4,194
To positive cash flow	6,525	3,132
Accounted for by increase in interest charge	£ 2,212	£ 1,062
Tax payable on year 6		£ 3,393

TABLE B — See paragraph 3.63

		Rent receivable immediately before beginning of quarter	Outstanding borrowing at beginning of quarter	Interest payable at end of quarter	Outstanding borrowing at end of quarter
Year 1 1	Q1	£(7,100)	£92,900	£ 3,251	£96,151
	Q2	(7,100)	89,051	3,117	92,168
	Q3	(7,100)	85,068	2,977	88,045
	Q4	(7,100)	80,945	2,833	83,778
				£12,178	
Year 2	Q1	(7,100)	76,678	2,684	79,362
	Q2	(7,100)	72,262	2,529	74,791
	Q3	(7,100)	67,691	2,369	70,060
	Q4	(7,100)	62,960	2,204	65,164
				£ 9,786	
Year 3	Q1	(7,100)	58,064	2.613	60,677
	Q2	(7,100)	53,577	2,411	55,988
	Q3	(7,100)	48,888	2,200	51,088
	Q4	(7,100)	43,988	1,979	45,967
				£ 9,203	
Year 4	Q1	(7,100)	38,867	1,749	40,616
	Q2	(7,100)	33,516	1,508	35,024
	Q3	(7,100)	27,924	1,257	29,181
	Q4	(7,100)	22,081	994	23,075
				£ 5,508	
Year 5	Q1	(7,100)	15,975	719	16,694
	Q2	(7,100)	9,594	432	10,026
	Q3	(7,100)	2,926	132	3,058
	Q4	(7,100)	(4,042)	(101)	(4,143)
				£ 1,182	
Year 6			Tax	£ 2,154	(1,989)

Non-Tax based lease

Interest payable 3½% per quarter for first two years, then rising to 4½% per quarter for remainder of lease.

	Pre-tax	Post-tax
Cash flow has changed from the original position to positive cash flow	£ 8,737 4,143	£ 4,194 1,989
Accounted for by increase in interest charge	£ 4,594	£ 2,205
Tax payable in year 6		£ 2,154

TABLE C – See paragraph 3.63

Recalculation of apportionment of gross income for investment period purposes into years 3, 4 and 5—on basis of data set out on Table B, namely change in interest payable rate to 4½% per quarter throughout those years.

	Outstanding borrowing			Gross income Apportioned
Year 1 Q1	£ 96,151			
Q2	92,168			
		Giving	**(Year 1**	£15,262
... and so on ...		**Apportionment**		
Year 2 Q3	70,060	**of Income**	**(Year 2**	12,264
Q4	65,164		**(Sub total**	£27,526
	£649,519			
Anticipated total to Year 5 Q2	£991,007			
Year 3 Q1	60,677			
Q2	55,988	**Giving**	**(Year 3**	8,329
		Apportionment		
... and so on ...		**of Income**	**(Year 4**	**4,984**
Year 5 Q2	10,026		**(Year 5**	1,161
Q3	3,058			
	£371,394		**(Sub total**	£14,474

TABLE D – See paragraph 3.78

		Rent receivable immediately before beginning of quarter	Tax payable (receivable) at beginning of quarter	Outstanding borrowing at beginning of quarter	Interest payable (receivable) at end of quarter	Outstanding borrowing at end of quarter
Year 1	Q1	(7,100)		92,900	3,251	96,151
	Q2	(7,100)		89,051	3,117	92,168
	Q3	(7,100)		85,068	2,977	88,045
	Q4	(7,100)		80,945	2,833	83,778
					£12,178	
Year 2	Q1	(7,100)		76,678	2,684	79,362
	Q2	(7,100)		72,262	2,529	74,791
	Q3	(7,100)		67,691	2,369	70,060
	Q4	(7,100)	(43,565)	19,395	679	20,074
					£ 8,261	
Year 3	Q1	(7,100)		12,974	454	13,428
	Q2	(7,100)		6,328	222	6,550
	Q3	(7,100)		(550)	(14)	(564)
	Q4	(7,100)	11,076	3,412	119	3,531
					£ 781	
Year 4	Q1	(7,100)		(3,569)	(89)	(3,658)
	Q2	(7,100)		10,758	(269)	(11,027)
	Q3	(7,100)		(18,127)	(453)	(18,580)
	Q4	(7,100)	15,190	(10,490)	(262)	(10,752)
					£(1,073)	
Year 5	Q1	(7,100)		(17,852)	(446)	(18,293)
	Q2	(7,100)		(25,398)	(635)	(26,033)
	Q3	(7,100)		(33,133)	(828)	(33,961)
	Q4	(7,100)	16,210	(24,851)	(621)	(25,472)
					£(2,530)	
Year 6	Q4		17,011			(8,461)

Tax based lease

Tax rate increases from 52% to 55% for profits taxable in respect of years, 2, 3, 4 and 5.

Cash flow has changed from positive	11,843
to a positive	8.461
	3,382
This represents: increase in tax liabilites	3,093
increase in interest payable	289
	£ 3,382

TABLE E — See paragraph 3.83

		Rent receivable immediately before beginning of quarter	Outstanding borrowing at beginning of quarter	Interest Payable	Dividend	Outstanding borrowing at end of quarter
Year 1	Q1	£(7,100)	£92,900	£ 3,251		£96,151
	Q2	(7,100)	89,051	3,117		92,168
	Q3	(7,100)	85,068	2,977		88,045
	Q4	(7,100)	79,945	2,833	1,000	84,778
				£12,178		
Year 2	Q1	(7,100)	77,678	2,719		80,397
	Q2	(7,100)	73,297	2,565		75,862
	Q3	(7,100)	68,762	2,407		71,169
	Q4	(7,100)	64,069	2,242	1,000	67,311
				£ 9,933		
Year 3	Q1	(7,100)	60,211	2,107		62,318
	Q2	(7,100)	55,218	1,933		57,151
	Q3	(7,100)	50,051	1,752		51,803
	Q4	(7,100)	44,703	1,565	1,000	47,268
				£ 7,357		
Year 4	Q1	(7,100)	40,168	1,406		41,574
	Q2	(7,100)	34,373	1,206		35,680
	Q3	(7,100)	28,580	1,000		29,580
	Q4	(7,100)	22,480	787	1,000	24,267
				£ 4,399		
Year 5	Q1	(7,100)	17,167	601		17,768
	Q2	(7,100)	10,668	373		11,041
	Q3	(7,100)	3,941	138		4,079
	Q4	(7,100)	(3,021)	(75)		(3,096)
				£ 1,037		

Non-tax based lease — tax ignored

£1,000 per annum withdrawn from lease by way of dividend
Interest payable 3½% per quarter throughout

Cash flow has changed from positive	£ 8,737
to positive	3,096
	5,641
Of this movement the dividends account for	4,000
and increase in interest charge, for the remainder	£ 1,641

TABLE F – See paragraph 3.84

Recalculation of apportionment of gross income for investment period purposes over all the years—on the basis of the data set out in Table E namely the withdrawal of dividends of £1,000 per annum in each of the first four years.

		Cash invested at quarter end			Gross income apportioned
Year 1	Q1	£ 96,151	Giving	Year 1	£14,607
	Q2	92,168	Apportionment	2	11,921
	... and so on...		of Income	3	8,839
Year 5	Q2	11.041		4	5,303
	Q4	4,079		5	1,330
		£1038,410			£42,000

TABLE G – See paragraph 3.88

		Rent receivable immediately before beginning of quarter	Outstanding borrowing at beginning of quarter	Interest payable at end of quarter on internal funds		Interest payable at end of quarter on external funds	Outstanding borrowing at end of quarter
Year 1	Q1	(7,100)	92,900	464		2,439	95,803
	Q2	(7,100)	88,703	443		2,328	91,474
	Q3	(7,100)	84,374	422		2,215	87,011
	Q4	(7,100)	79,911	400		2,098	82,409
				1,729	£ 10,809	9,080	
Year 2	Q1	(7,100)	75,309	376		1,977	77,662
	Q2	(7,100)	70,562	353		1,852	72,767
	Q3	(7,100)	65,667	328		1,724	67,719
	Q4	(7,100)	60,619	303		1,591	62,513
				1,360	£ 8,504	7,144	
Year 3	Q1	(7,100)	55,413	277		1,454	57,144
	Q2	(7,100)	50,044	250		1,314	51,608
	Q3	(7,100)	44,508	223		1,168	45,899
	Q4	(7,100)	38,799	194		1,018	40,011
				944	£ 5,898	4,954	
Year 4	Q1	(7,100)	32,911	165		864	33,940
	Q2	(7,100)	26,840	134		705	27,679
	Q3	(7,100)	20,579	103		540	21,222
	Q4	(7,100)	14,122	71		371	14,564
				473	£ 2,953	2,480	
Year 5	Q1	(7,100)	7,464	37		196	7,697
	Q2	(7,100)	597	3		16	616
	Q3	(7,100)	(6,484)		(162)		(6,646)
	Q4	(7,100)	(13,746)		(344)		(14,090)
				40	(506)	212	
					£ (254)		

Lease–calculations ignore tax.

Interest on funds from internal sources (one ¼ of total) at 2% per quarter.
On external funds (three quarters) at 3½% per quarter

Cash flow has changed from positive	£ 8,737
to positive	14,090
Representing decrease in interest charge	£ 5,353

TABLE H – See paragraph 3.88

Recalculation of apportionment of gross into years 3, 4 and 5 on basis of data set out in Table G, namely interest rate on internal funds of 2% per quarter.

		Outstanding borrowing				Gross Income Apportioned
Year 1	1st quarter	95,803	)	Giving	(Year 1	15,976
	2nd quarter	91,474	)		(Year 2	12,570
	... and so on ...		)	Apportion-ment	(Year 3	8,719
			)	of	(	
Year 5	1st Quarter	7,697	)	income	(Year 4	4,363
	2nd quarter	616	)		(Year 5	372
		£937,738				£42,000

INDEX